100 Group Games

Skills in Facilitating Group Games

100 GROUP GAMES

Skills in Facilitating Group Games

Edited by
Ping Kwong KAM

ISBN: 978-962-937-641-3

Published by
    City University of Hong Kong Press
    Tat Chee Avenue
    Kowloon, Hong Kong
    Website: www.cityu.edu.hk/upress
    E-mail: upress@cityu.edu.hk

Printed in Hong Kong

Contents

Section 2 Mutual Understanding Games

Section 3 Group Cooperation and Cohesion Games

Section 4 Problem-solving Games

List of Tables and Figures

Foreword

The ability of human beings to both understand the world and also to learn how to accomplish new tasks with skill remains both a magical and mysterious attribute of our species. Throughout history, we have found new and exciting ways to help new generations acquire cultural knowledge and build their skill repertoire. Telling people how to do a task is unlikely to engender the skill necessary to complete that same task reliably at a future date, unless the skill is rehearsed and practiced. In social work, internships and field placement have become the central vehicles for learning the required skills for professional practice in a protected environment, and the same principle holds good for other health and caring professions. This inspiring book, edited by Dr Ping Kwong Kam, provides a valuable resource that can be used both as part of the learning process during an internship or fieldwork placement in an agency or as a teaching resource in a classroom. The book is a very valuable contribution to the resources available to teachers and fieldwork educators, particularly in contexts where students are engaged in working with groups, and also as a resource for social workers and youth workers engaged in group work practice, particularly with adolescents. Unusually, the book provides a source both of material for a teacher's own teaching and also of exercises that students and practitioners can use in their group work practice.

A key strength of this book is that it has been developed by teachers in collaboration with students. This highly unusual aspect of the book both gives voice to students and demonstrates the commitment of the authors to collaborative learning. This collaborative element has generated a number of innovative games that provide an exciting and imaginative way to initiate, continue, and maintain the learning process.

While the games in the book are rightly grounded in the cultural tradition from which they originate, it is remarkable how easily they translate to other cultural contexts. Boldly, this speaks to the commonalities and similarities across different cultural groups rather than their differences. There are a small number of games which may need modification and be transposed into a different cultural context before use. The authors do not shy away from such difficult issues. Some games involve touch and would not be suitable automatically for all ethnic groups or in mixed gender groups without careful thought by the teacher. Some of the games are genuinely innovative, some are traditional group work games. Hence, this book provides a compendium of both traditional group work games as well as new and innovative additions to the genre.

Professor Steven M Shardlow,

Professor Emeritus of Social Work, Keele University, UK
Editor-in-Chief, The Journal of Social Work

Foreword

In many ways, group work is a relatively neglected and inadequately acknowledged modality in social work practice. As a long-time group worker and group work teacher, I am excited by Dr. Kam's book project—*100 Group Games: Skills in Facilitating Group Games*. I have seen the earlier Chinese edition of the book as well, which is a remarkable success in Hong Kong and East Asia. It obviously addresses learning needs among social work practitioners and students, and I am excited to see the English translation in print. Practitioners and social work students are often looking for specific games or exercises for a wide range of group practice situations, and the breadth of the book's scope offers a rich range of options.

Teaching of group work is often organized according to the type and function of the group, and this book is organized topically to address specific group tasks such as warm-up or ice-breaking, mutual understanding, group cooperation and cohesion, and problem solving. Practitioners, as well as instructors and students, will find the games very relevant and helpful, and most of them can also be used as in class exercises or illustration. The book, as an extremely accessible resource, is likely to be valued by social work colleagues in different parts of the world. Through my extensive training and consultation work in Canada and internationally, colleagues in frontline practice often ask for game ideas and instructions that they can readily apply in their day-to-day practice. I expect many of these colleagues will find the book handy.

It is a privilege to be invited to write this foreword for Dr. Kam's book, which is a solid, well-organized, and high-quality resource for social work colleagues, students, and instructors. It is a welcome addition to the professional literature on social work with groups, and will likely enhance the advancement of group work practice in many parts of the world.

Professor Adolf Ka Tat Tsang,
Professor, Factor-Inwentash Faculty of Social Work
University of Toronto, Canada

Preface

Making good use of group games is immensely beneficial in group practice, as games help drive engagement, foster the mood, achieve goals, and ultimately promote the group's development. If group facilitators are able to grow their game portfolio and keep enhancing their game facilitation skills, they will surely make every group more lively, vibrant, and motivated. For this reason, game facilitation skills have been part of my social work teaching routine at City University of Hong Kong. Whenever appropriate and possible, I would leverage games in class to help students get to know each other, build relationships, and drive their engagement in the course, while at the same time demonstrating how games can be facilitated in a group environment. I also offer students the opportunity to run warm-up games, share my experience in facilitating and leveraging group games, and encourage them to keep looking for more suitable games.

Together with my social work students, I have built a collection of over 100 games to help social work practitioners and students systematically acquire game facilitation skills and boost their confidence in game facilitation. These games have all been tried with the students and modified accordingly. Many students, who later applied these games in their social work fieldwork practicum training, have confirmed their suitability and practicality. Frontline social workers and social work graduates who have adopted our collection of games have found that they are not only suitable for facilitating local group activities, but they are also useful for training other facilitators of group activities.

In light of this positive feedback and encouragement, I decided to turn our collective effort into a book. In 2009, the Chinese edition was published by the City University of Hong Kong Press. In addition to our collection of games, the book also included four theory-focused essays detailing the concept, practice sharing, and application skills of group game facilitation, which are covered in the first section. The first essay is my reflection on the key elements of facilitating group games. In the second essay, Mr Yau Kuen Lau illustrates the briefing and facilitation skills in group games, giving readers a systematic look at every meticulous step of game facilitation and the art behind it. The third essay is by Mr Kwok Wing Chan and focuses on the debriefing skills in group games, underscoring the importance and essence of the "debrief" during group games. In the fourth essay, Mr Fai Kuen Leung discusses the risk assessment and precautions of group game facilitation, making it clear to readers that game facilitation is a painstaking task that requires careful planning and safety rules. The second section of this book provides the details for 100 practical group games. These are grouped into four categories: (1) warm-up and ice-breaking, (2) mutual understanding, (3) group cooperation and cohesion, and (4) problem solving. The collection was built on the contributions of 43 social work students and my own game repertoire. I have since systematically organised, edited, expanded, trimmed, and supplemented the details of the games with appropriate revisions and compilation.

The response to the Chinese edition of this book has been overwhelming. Many social workers and group workers found the games included in the book to be simple and easy to understand, practical, and vastly suitable for application in group work and team activities. I have also been invited to hold group game skills training workshops in Hong Kong, Mainland China, and overseas on multiple occasions to share the concepts, skills, and experience of group game facilitation, and to demonstrate how to effectively facilitate the games outlined in the book. In addition to the positive and encouraging feedback from local participants, non-Chinese participants in overseas training workshops have been equally enthusiastic as they pointed out that the games demonstrated are very suitable for facilitating local group activities and most of them could be easily adapted to multinational settings (though in some settings, certain games involving direct physical contact would have to be revised for religious reasons). The only downside that has been voiced is that many of these participants do not read Chinese, preventing them from using the book as a practical reference beyond the workshop.

Thus, to allow this book to be used in other locations, I have compiled this English edition, titled *100 Group Games: Skills in facilitating Group Games*, to be published by the City University of Hong Kong Press. In addition to translating the original work into English, I have also revised or removed some colloquial terms and wordings bearing cultural differences to ensure it is appropriate for an overseas audience. As for the 100 games in the book, I have rewritten the names and modified the instructions with additional reminders and precautionary points to note in relation to cultural differences.

Now being available in English, I hope that overseas readers will continue to find the games useful. The book is written for social work students, inexperienced social workers, and game facilitators in English-speaking countries as well as social workers in Hong Kong working with ethnic minority groups who can speak English but cannot understand Chinese. To meet the needs of these target groups, this book is not intended to be just a game manual. It also serves the purpose of helping to equip readers with the basic knowledge and skills necessary for facilitating group games as well as to provide them with useful and practical games for use in their daily practice. This is one characteristic that helps distinguish this book from other games manuals. The English version also includes the first four theory-focused chapters to provide an overview of the important concepts, knowledge, and practice skills required to facilitate group games before they start to use the games in the book. These essays emphasise the lessons drawn from the authors' practical experience and detail the most important points to bear in mind during game facilitation.

Of the target readership outlined above, social work students will find it particularly relevant and helpful for undertaking their fieldwork practicum training as the majority of the 100 games in the book can be used in a variety of group work contexts in western countries. Since this book was developed as a collaborative venture with my social work students, all the games have been tested and were found to be suitable for use by social work students. Further, social work practitioners are often looking for more new and specific games to address specific group tasks such as warm-ups or ice-breaking, mutual understanding, group cooperation and cohesion, and problem solving, so this book will offer additional practice resources for these individuals. The book is also a valuable teaching resource for social work teachers and fieldwork educators in social work programmes in western countries and can be used with students in class exercises or demonstrations as well as during fieldwork practicum teaching. While this is certainly not the only book on the market illustrating group games, the games included in this book share a unique feature—each of them can be carried out with simple and easy-to-find tools or materials, or no extra materials at all. Each game has been tried repeatedly and modified when necessary. Many of the games are illustrated with pictures to show how it should be facilitated, helping readers to master every step of facilitation precisely. Taken together, this book marries the theory and practice of group game facilitation in a way that will appeal to a global audience.

This English edition has only been made possible by the full assistance and support from City University of Hong Kong Press. Special thanks to Miss Cherry Sze and Miss Joli Kam for their preliminary English translation of some of the games in this book. I would like to express my sincere gratitude to Steven Shardlow (Professor Emeritus of Social Work, Keele University, UK) and Adolf Ka Tat Tsang (Professor of the Factor-Inwentash Faculty of Social Work, University of Toronto, Canada) for writing the forewords to this book.

Lastly, I would like to dedicate this book to my peers around the globe who are enthusiastic and proactive in promoting group games. I hope our efforts will not only bring joy to people from all walks of life but also foster transformation and growth of individuals and enable groups to develop in a healthy way.

Ping Kwong Kam
April 2022

Part I
Concepts and Practice

Key Elements of Facilitating Group Games

Ping Kwong Kam

Introduction

To be an outstanding facilitator or host in leading group games, in addition to possessing extensive knowledge and proficient skills, the most important thing is to accumulate a vast amount of experience. Since group games are experiential activities, every game a facilitator leads offers distinct experiences, lessons, and conclusions. Through the accumulation of different experiences, it is possible to develop a deep understanding of game functions and learn more about our own leading style. Constant self-reflection and sharing will also help to develop a better grasp of the key elements of leading group games. This chapter focuses on exploring the three key elements of leading group games, including the functions of group games, essential qualities of the facilitator, and common methods of leading games.

Functions of group games

Games have many positive functions in group activities (Kroehnert, 2002; Lindsay & Orton, 2008; Scannell & Scannell, 2010; Shalaev et al., 2019). They have been shown to:

1. adjust the body and mind, evoke pleasant feelings and emotions;

2. help group members warm up and participate more actively in group activities;

3. "break the ice" and reduce unfamiliarity and defensiveness among group members;

4. facilitate mutual understanding between group members and provide more opportunities for group members to interact;

5. build up relationships among group members;

6. promote team spirit, communication, and cohesion of the group;

7. facilitate the growth and development of the group and its members; and

8. enhance problem solving and self-awareness skills of group members and promote their personal growth.

In addition to these functions, group games can also be used to help build relationships between the facilitator and participants, enhance knowledge of others in the group, and encourage the group to focus on the "theme" of their meeting. These benefits are discussed below.

Building relationships between the group facilitator and group members

Not only can group games help build relationships among group members, but it can also establish closer relationships between the group facilitator and the participants during the games. The group facilitator is usually viewed by the group members as an authority figure with a higher status. This is particularly pronounced during the early stages of the meeting when group members are unfamiliar with the facilitator and thus avoid taking the initiative to communicate with them. However, playing games with the group members more frequently helps break the ice between the two parties. The joyful and pleasant atmosphere brought about by games can easily bring everyone closer, allowing the facilitator to mingle with the group members more quickly.

Enhancing knowledge about each group member

Group members naturally reveal their most authentic qualities during the games. Games provide ample opportunities for facilitators to learn about the personalities of the group members, characteristics of how they get along with the others, communication methods, and leadership abilities. Therefore, the facilitator should ensure that they observe the performance of each team member during the game. If the facilitator can increase group members' participation in the game during the early stage of their meeting or activity, then they will be able to more quickly and comprehensively grasp the characteristics of each group member. Doing so will also be helpful in increasing group members' participation in future group activities and provide cues for handling the group dynamics in non-game activities, as well as helping the facilitator design other suitable group games and activities.

Focusing on the theme of the group meeting

In addition to helping group members warm up, break the ice, get to know each other, and establish relationships, games can also bring out the theme of group meetings naturally. For example, after group members have played the game "Weave a spider web" (see Game 44 in this book), they are often more conscious of needing to establish and use a "supportive network" later in the meeting or non-game activities. Presenting a theme using games encourages group members to participate sooner and establishes trust and confidence, making the rest of the meeting and non-game activities proceed more smoothly as well as helping the facilitator to effectively and confidently achieve the group meeting objectives.

Qualities of the game facilitator

While playing group games can be immensely beneficial, whether a game is successful and well-received depends heavily upon the skills and personality of the game facilitator. While briefing/debriefing and leadership skills can often be developed through study and experience, the facilitator can also enhance the success of the game by possessing the following positive characteristics or qualities.

The facilitator should enjoy playing the game

The most important quality of a game facilitator is not their proficient and lively skills, but rather, the facilitator's genuine pleasure in the game they are leading. If they genuinely enjoy playing the game, no matter how many times they have played it, then they will still enjoy leading it and will find new pleasure every time. This joy has a huge contagious effect on the group members (Le Fevre, 2002). The group members can sense that their facilitator is not leading the game as a work responsibility but that they are interested in the participants and outcome. This can greatly increase participation. Therefore, the facilitator must treat each leading opportunity as a new experience and bring positive energy to the game every time.

The facilitator should enjoy playing with the group members

Many game facilitators think that their sole responsibility is to clearly explain the steps and rules of the game, and then let the group members play it, acting only as an observer with minimal interaction with the group. However, in addition to their role as a referee and encouraging participation at the start of the game, an outstanding facilitator should also join the group members and play the game with them. Doing so offers many benefits. For instance, playing the game with the group will allow the facilitator to better determine if all the group members understand the rules of the game. Facilitator participation creates a sense of equality and collective spirit, and establishes a relationship between the facilitator and the group members, bringing everyone closer. It also allows the facilitator to learn about the characteristics and motivations of each group member while playing together and to boost group members' interest in the game as well as in subsequent non-game activities. Finally, the more the facilitator plays with the group members, the more they will feel welcomed and the easier it will be to get along with each other in other games and non-game activities.

The facilitator should strive to create a fun atmosphere

To avoid a dull game, the facilitator must set the ambiance and create a fun mood before and during the game. Not only does a game require the participation of group members (and the facilitator, as explained above), but it also requires the facilitator to sometimes create a humorous, amusing, exciting, or competitive atmosphere

while briefing/debriefing or in side conversations during the game, so as to increase the participation of group members and make the game more fun (Scannell & Scannell, 2010). However, the facilitator must intervene at appropriate times and must not assert too much influence while trying to create a good vibe. The facilitator should also not act like a machine when it comes to explaining the rules and making sure group members comply with them, but should instead be adept at igniting group members' passion for the game and act as a catalyst for participation. In addition to making sure group members are having fun, the facilitator also needs to remember to have fun in the game (which feeds back into the facilitator genuinely enjoying the game and the trickle-down effect this has on the group members).

Methods of facilitating group games

The qualities above will set the stage for the games. There are also other abilities and methods facilitators will develop with experience. Seven ideas and skills facilitators should consider are explained below.

Clearly identify the objective of the game before choosing it

Game facilitators usually arbitrarily choose a game that they have played and enjoyed playing before without first identifying the objective of the game, making "having fun" the primary consideration for choosing the game. While having fun is an essential aspect of game facilitation, it should not be the only criterion when choosing what game to play with a particular group. The facilitator needs to first figure out whether the game matches or achieves the group's objective, and only after deciding what this objective or message is can the most suitable game be chosen. This may involve some trial and error, with the facilitator making appropriate improvements to the chosen game after it is used in preparation for a similar situation in the future. Games that were fun in the past may not fully accommodate the current objective. Group games are just tools; if not used properly, they cannot and will not produce the desired results. Thus, game facilitators must spend some time and effort to clarify their objectives before designing and choosing a suitable game.

Games should not only be played at the beginning of a meeting

Many people believe games should only be played during the early stages of a group gathering or meeting as a way to help group members warm up, get to know each other, and build relationships. However, these functions are also needed at every other stage of the meeting. Since achieving the meeting objectives is typically an incremental process, instead of only having games in the beginning, it is best to have games at various stages to achieve the best result. This also relates to the theme of the meeting or that stage of the meeting. For example, while games at the start of a meeting may focus on warming up, some similar games should also be played in the middle of the meeting when group members start to show signs of tiredness or decreased concentration. These games can help them loosen up and relax, and to facilitate continued participation in the group activities. Before the meeting is over, different games can be used to help group members summarise their feelings and share the lessons they have learned from the meeting (not just during the games). These late-stage games can also help build support and boost morale of group members. Therefore, there is not a fixed formula stipulating when games must be played. The facilitator needs to be aware of changes in the objectives over the course of the meeting as well as the overall dynamics of the group members and then decide what games would be appropriate at those times. Similarly, when groups will have multiple meetings, games should not only be played at the first of these but would be beneficial at each subsequent meeting as well.

Determine when changes need to be made to a game

Regardless of how interesting a game is, once it has been played too many times, it will inevitably lose its novelty. Therefore, game facilitators should work hard to discover new games and rack their brains to design new activities. However, this does not always have to involve inventing something completely new. A game can often be "re-invented" by modifying the rules slightly, and with a little bit of creativity, facilitators can make the game more fun and novel again. For example, by changing the game "A big wind blows" into "A small wind blows" (see Game 19), the game increases in difficulty and will also boost group members' participation. Consequently, if game facilitators are able to make variations and add new features to the games they already use, then they will never have to worry about running out of games or about group members getting tired of the same games.

Modify the game according to the venue and characteristics of group members

Game design should be modified based on multiple elements, as the same game may not be suitable for every venue or target audience (Sheafor & Horejsi, 2003). Indeed, even a slight modification of a game may lead to surprising results. For example, it may not be possible to play the game "Finding the spy" (see Game 43), which requires members of the group to divide into teams and stand side by side, in a small room with only enough space to sit instead of stand. However, the game can be modified so that group members divided into two teams can sit side by side and raise their hands up (instead of standing) or keep them down (instead of squatting). Such changes to a game will allow group members to participate more actively, which can be very exciting. This modified game would also make it more suitable for elderly group members with reduced mobility. Therefore, the game facilitator must remember to keep the venue size and layout as well as the characteristics of group members in mind when choosing games.

Consider when to combine different games

In addition to changing or modifying a game, as described in the sections above, one of the best ways to alter or create a game is to combine two games into one. This method will not only add novelty to the game, but it will also make group members more eager to play it. For example, the games "Who's the Leader" (see Game 22) and "Musical Chairs" can be combined. Apart from being fun to play, the combination also increases the difficulty and challenge of the game. In fact, many games, including those in Part II of this book, can work well together. Obviously, the game facilitator must also be adept at handling the increased complexity and confusion that can arise by combining two different games. Facilitators should pay extra attention to the overlap in briefing and rules between the games and ensure that all group members understand these changes. It is also important to continually encourage group members to try harder in the new game, which may be more difficult. Again, it is important for such changes to be made based on the venue and characteristics of the group.

Games should be arranged in a good order

To effectively engage group members in the games and to elevate the overall mood of the meeting, the game facilitator must be proficient at arranging the order of games. Proper game sequencing makes it easier for group members to keep up with the pace of the games, assists the facilitator in explaining the rules more clearly, and is an effective way to liven up the games.

One method is to arrange the games in order of increasing difficulty. This allows group members to learn each step of a simple game, then slowly add more complicated or exciting steps or rules. It also helps group members to gradually build confidence as it involves games that build upon each other in a fun atmosphere. For example, before playing the typical version of "Trust rocking" (see Game 77), a similar game can first be played in teams of three, thus allowing group members to fully understand the objective and rules before playing the game in one big circle.

Another method is to follow one game with another relevant game. Grouping relevant games together gives the group members a sense of completing the games in a fluid motion. For example, after playing the game "Finding the spy" (see Game 43),

which involves dividing the group members into two teams facing each other in parallel lines, the facilitator should consider playing the game "Spider and snake" (see Game 9), which uses a similar set up.

Involve group members in designing or changing a game's rules

The game facilitator should not be the only person responsible for designing or changing the games. Instead, group members should also be invited to discuss the choice of games as well as the general tips they have that help them play (Elias et al., 2012). Group members should be encouraged to give comments or suggestions to change the rules of a game and if they think the game fits the desired objective. Indeed, group members can also be consulted early on to determine the underlying objective of the meeting and the games. When group members are given the opportunity to design the game, the effectiveness of the games will be enhanced (Tate, 2008), as they will be more inclined to participate, and the game will better meet their needs. For example, after playing the game "Body rock, paper, scissors" (see Game 10), the facilitator should encourage the group members to customise a set of movements or even facial expressions to represent "rock, paper, scissors". This also gives group members a sense of ownership over the game and a stake in its success.

Under certain circumstances, facilitators can also invite the more active group members (especially those who proposed appropriate changes to the game) to lead the rest of the group to play the modified game (Lindsay & Lindsay, 2008). In such situations, the game facilitator does not have supreme authority in leading the games but should consider releasing some responsibility to be shared with the group members at appropriate times. Working together with them as partners, in addition to also playing the games with them, will make the game more fun and enhance the relationship between the facilitator and group members. It will also help better match the games with group members' interests and the underlying objectives of the meeting. When playing games geared towards team building, allowing group members to set challenges or targets by themselves, such as to complete a task within a certain time period, can ignite the group members' desire to participate more in the game as well as in non-game activities. The game facilitator should, therefore, create the appropriate atmosphere to unleash and make use of the creativity and abilities of the group members, so that they can have an opportunity to maximise their potential and contribute to the group's success.

Conclusion

The use of games is an essential group facilitation skill. Proper use of games can encourage group members' participation, help achieve group activity objectives, promote team development, and make the team feel more lively, energetic, and motivated. However, for games to be successful, the game facilitator should master the key elements of leading games, understand the functions that games serve, and clearly identify the objectives of the activity before choosing the most suitable game. In addition, the game facilitator should explore the fun side of the games, cultivate joy when playing the games, and be willing to share their feelings about the games with the group members. Most importantly, facilitators must constantly remind themselves to be flexible in the face of changing circumstances. They should learn how to modify games in a flexible manner, combine different games, arrange games in a proper sequence, and frequently exchange views with other group members. Since games are activities that require group members to participate and experience, the facilitator must try to remember these key concepts of "experiential learning". Besides accumulating more experience, facilitators and group members should also constantly reflect and observe the process and outcomes of the game (Chung, 2002). Doing so will be helpful to improve the games as well as the facilitator's leadership skills.

References

Elias, G.S., Garfield, R., & Gutschera, K.R. (2012). *Characteristics of games*. The MIT Press.

Kroehnert, G. (2002). *Games trainers play outdoors*. McGraw-Hill.

Le Fevre, D.N. (2002). *Best new games*. Human Kinetics.

Lindsay, T., & Orton, S. (2008). *Group work practice in social work*. Learning Matters.

Scannell, M., & Scannell, E.E. (2010). *The big book of team motivation games*. McGraw-Hill.

Shalaev, V., Emelyanov, F., & Shalaeva, S. (2019). Social functions of games in modern society: Educational perspectives. *Advances in Social Sciences, Education and Humanities Research, 396*, 192–197.

Sheafor, B.W., & Horejsi, C.R. (2003). *Techniques and guidelines for social work practice* (6th ed.). Pearson Education.

Tate, M.L. (2008). *Engage the Brain Games*. Cron Press.

2

Facilitation and Briefing Skills for Group Games

Yau Kuen Lau

Introduction

While games can be considered play in some cases, they typically involve much more than just playing. When we play a game, we play by certain rules. Games not only provide entertainment that helps strike an emotional and psychological balance, they can also foster interpersonal relationships and cooperation between participants, and even promote self-awareness, self-understanding, and personal growth.

Game facilitation concepts and techniques have been gaining attention over the years, leading many to wonder how to use games more effectively in certain activities. The primary goal in learning game facilitation skills goes beyond simply learning how to run a game smoothly to instead focus on bringing about a positive outcome for participants. This chapter discusses game facilitation and briefing techniques, including game preparation, facilitator engagement, and collaborative growth. Important points that have been drawn from years of game facilitation experience are also outlined and demonstrated using several example games.

Carefully prepared and meticulously designed

Successful game facilitation is inherently derived from good game preparation. There are three main considerations when preparing a game: group characteristics, necessary materials, and purpose.

Choose the right games based on the target group's characteristics

Children cannot hold their attention for too long. To keep them engaged, it is advisable for the game facilitator to choose simpler games. Adolescents prefer fresh and exciting group activities, so novel, competitive, and challenging games will suit them well. Games involving high levels of critical thinking or difficulty are more suitable for adults. Elderly participants may require games that require less movement. Furthermore, when designing games for a newly formed group, the facilitator also needs to consider whether some interactions, such as those between opposite sexes, will cause group members to feel embarrassed or uncomfortable. In such cases, it may be necessary to plan games that minimise unnecessary physical contact.

Prepare activity materials and test them in advance

When designing a game, facilitators must have a thorough understanding of the venue and facilities, taking into account their nature and characteristics. Props prepared for the games must be of an appropriate size, weight, and complexity that is suitable for the target participants and venue.

Understand the purposes and objectives of the games

Entry-level games create a relaxed and lively atmosphere to enable participants to loosen up. Advanced-level games aim to consciously guide and inspire interpersonal exchanges and promote the social development of participants, such as communication games and trust-building games. The game facilitator should determine the objective of the meeting and the purpose of each game in advance in addition to familiarising themselves with the rules and precautions of each game to ensure that the game fits the intended objective and runs smoothly.

Be an engaging facilitator and pay attention to the techniques

The following sections include tips for facilitators. These deal with both characteristics the facilitator should have as well as ways to prepare for certain situations.

Be confident and open

If the game is one where participants are supposed to have child-like fun, the facilitator should tap into their inner child by speaking and acting like one to fully engage the participants, evoking their childhood memories and youthful joy. It is perfectly fine to be silly in order to get the group members to feel more comfortable doing so as well.

Clearly explain the rules and go over the top in game demonstration

Explain the rules of each game step-by-step. Each step should be concise and clear. It would be best if the rules are explained from the perspective of the participants. The facilitator must also draw participants' attention to any safety issues or precautions. They should also demonstrate the game properly with generous and excessive body movements. It is important to move around and be extra expressive when explaining the rules to ensure participants understand what is required. The verbal explanation and exaggerated demonstration lay the foundation for the game and will help to achieve the desired results.

Respect individual will and do not coerce participation

Never coerce group members to participate in a game. Forced participation will upset participants and even create a confrontational mood, violating the key principles of game facilitation and thwarting the underlying purpose of the game. The facilitator needs to respect each member's free will and only encourage them to play or re-join the game when appropriate, turning them from an onlooker into a participant.

Properly handle the competitiveness of the game

Games provide a valuable opportunity for introspection, particularly with regard to interactions with others. While some games focus on group connection and have no clear "winner", others use healthy competition to motivate group members. Facilitators should guide participants to deal with competition in the game with the right attitude. The key is for participants to be fully involved. Facilitators should help them focus on having fun and fulfilling the purpose of the game regardless of their success. "Losses" can be equally as helpful in this as they provide a chance to sort out what went wrong. Facilitators must also be sure to monitor any issues with the participants' understanding of the rules.

Understand when to use a game and how much time is needed

Depending on the needs of the group, facilitators should use their experience to decide when to use a game and which game would be best. However, this does not need to be a set schedule. For example, if participants seem to be losing energy, then the facilitator can insert a warm-up game to excite them before returning to the meeting or switching to a more complex game. This requires an in-depth understanding of the games and how long they take. By inserting and varying the games in this way, participants will be less likely to get bored or exhausted.

Attentive counselling, collaborative growth

In addition to running activities smoothly, the most important goal of a game facilitator is to drive the personal growth of participants as part of the group and counsel them towards a specific outcome. By following the five stages of group development—warm-up, interaction, cohesion, problem solving, and sharing upon conclusion—a facilitator can foster engagement to enable group members to communicate effectively and enhance mutual trust. Group members will also be more willing to contribute their efforts to completing tasks and resolving problems they encounter in the game. However, these efforts can be enhanced if the facilitator uses a debriefing session after the game to recognise and praise the participants for their work. Without this, all or some of the group members may feel that they are not valued and may lose trust in the group, thus undermining group development.

Interaction between game participants in a group is vital. The facilitator should support and encourage group members, particularly those lacking self-confidence and avoiding participation, to express

themselves, thus bolstering their engagement and interaction with other group members. The facilitator should also apply interactive skills when appropriate. For instance, group members should be guided to take a positive and constructive approach in their group interaction to foster a sense of security and mutual trust. In this, the facilitator must be genuine. Empty talk does nothing to facilitate a smooth game and will not help achieve the purpose of the game. A facilitator should apply techniques with care and consideration, and avoid becoming robotic in their explanations, demonstrations, and debriefing. Experienced facilitators often run the risk of losing passion for the games after getting very familiar with the procedures and serving in the same job for years. Some facilitators also focus solely on the growth of participants and overlook their own needs and introspection. In these situations, facilitators fail to grow with the participants. Facilitators should pursue self-improvement through the activities they organise because counselling is not just about helping others, but it is also about helping ourselves. The games are meant to enhance the group as a whole.

Examples of facilitation and briefing skills for ice-breaking and warm-up games

Some mini-games can be used for breaking the ice and warming up. Such games can help participants to engage in the group activities as soon as possible, allowing a closer relationship between the facilitator and participants to be established faster, while also fostering mutual trust. There are several tips that facilitators should bear in mind.

1. Use quizzes, mini-games, simple magic tricks, or IQ games to make initial contact with the game participants.

2. Take the initiative to talk to participants who arrive early; introduce yourself and use this time to try to better understanding their expectations for the activity and meeting in general.

3. Observe carefully and listen proactively; pay attention to how the participants interact

during the game. Is this interaction sufficient to achieve the objectives of the group? Encourage engagement and respond with appreciation when appropriate.

4. Carefully monitor each person's performance, participation, and initiative during the game. This will serve as a baseline reference for assessing changes in their participation level throughout the activity or meeting. Do some group members respond better to certain games? Does anyone appear uncomfortable? Use this information to render targeted facilitation and drive their engagement as soon as possible.

5. Allow participants who are not as capable or motivated to fall behind without making this a spectacle; they may simply need some time to adapt. Always remember that a game is "a challenge by choice". Check in with them to see if they require assistance or for the rules to be explained again.

These tips are further exemplified using several example games in the following sections. These include games with and without tools to give a full picture of what is required of facilitators in each style.

Games with Tools

Example 1: Chicken thrower

Tools:

1. Five to six rubber chickens or any stuffed toys slightly larger than the palms of the participants' hands

2. Stickers (for group members to write their names or titles)

How to play:

1. After requesting the group to sit in a circle, ask each group member to give their name (and title, if applicable).

2. Explain the rules of the game:

   i. Make eye contact with a group member

   ii. Call the name of that group member

   iii. Throw the toy to the group member whose name you called

   iv. Every group member only has one chance to catch the toy

   v. The last catcher throws the toy back to the facilitator

   vi. Each group member will throw the toy to the same person in each round

3. For additional details, see Game 35 in Part II of this book.

Facilitation and briefing:

1. Choice of prop: Rubber chickens are fun and colourful. These characteristics will help engage the participants. Any toy can be used to serve this purpose. Before explaining the rules, take out the stuffed toy or rubber chicken and ask: "Is anyone scared by this toy? Will anyone be unable to touch the toy?" If yes, replace this with another toy deemed acceptable by the group members. The intention here is to understand the needs of each group member and express the facilitator's care and respect of these needs. It also provides a foundation to build a relationship with group members. This should be done for all types of toys used in the game (i.e., not all five or six toys are the same).

2. Setting up: When inviting group members to tell their names, encourage everyone to pay attention to the names of other group members. If someone forgets the name of another group member while playing the game, help them to remember or ask the other group member to repeat it. There is no need to force them to remember the names of all group members and there should be no "penalty" or embarrassment for forgetting.

3. Explaining the rules: Plan the specific order of the rules in advance before explaining them. Some games require a specific sequence of rules, while others are more fluid. Use a logical order for that

specific game. This is also the time to use exaggerated movements to demonstrate the rules. For example, the instructions to "make eye contact", "call the name of that group member", and "throw the toy to the group member whose name you called" should be given in the right order and demonstrated with obvious actions.

4. Play the game: Invite the group members to start throwing the toy. Timing is not the main focus in the first round, though you can urge them to speed up. This timing can be changed starting in the second round and prior to the third round, you may ask: "How can you do it faster?" By the fourth round, set a shorter time for them as a goal. Note that the throwing order must follow that of the first round without changes, so each person is throwing to the same group member each time. It may be good to indicate this to the group participants to avoid confusion. The idea is to use indirect intervention while the game is being played instead of telling participants what to do. This gives the participants the sense that you are there to assist and support them rather than acting as an authority. Asking how they think they can throw better or faster allows them to solve problems together. If there are no responses to this, then suggest that maybe they can move their chairs or stand closer together so they can quickly toss the toys to each other. However, try any strategies they offer first.

5. Adding difficulty: When starting the fifth round, add additional toys and say "We're increasing the level of difficulty this time. You need to keep throwing all the toys I'm holding to your group members one by one in the same order. So each time you catch a toy, you must quickly throw it to the next person or you'll end up with toys all over!" This is a technique to add complexity to the game as well as push for more active engagement.

6. Debriefing: After playing the game, stress that it was meant to break the ice and let them get to know each other. The game has no winners or losers, but now is a good time to ask participants to compare how they felt in different rounds and what they learned each time.

7. Notes for the facilitator: Ice-breaking games like this offer an opportunity to observe the participants' abilities as well as their physical and mental states. Be sure to observe how group members react to the changes in speed and the added challenges. Use this time to identify any outspoken group members and those who may need extra motivating. Games that involve saying the name of each participant will also help you (and other group members) remember everyone's names. Keep in mind that the group members could be meeting for the first time. The meeting may involve something entirely new for them. It could, therefore, be stressful for them to go out of their comfort zone. Using this kind of game, which will in most cases result in a little chaos as the speed and number of toys increases, is one way to help put participants at ease and get them physically and mentally ready for the meeting or activity they are there to participate in.

Example 2: Balancing nails

Tools:

Fourteen 160-mm iron nails (per team)

How to play:

1. Invite the participants to form teams with three to four people each.

2. Distribute 14 nails to each team.

3. Instruct them to balance 13 nails on the head of the 14th nail. No other tools are allowed.

Facilitation and briefing:

1. Choice of prop: Be sure that the nails are clean and avoid any unnecessary risk.

2. Setting up and explaining the rules: Allow them to organise their own teams. When inviting the team members to work together to complete the challenge, be specific in the instructions.

3. Playing the game: Allow the participants to discuss solutions in their groups for a few minutes. It may also be necessary to give some hints, such as "Why did I give you a long nail but not a piece of iron bar? What's the difference between a nail and an iron bar?" If the teams are still unable to complete the task one to two minutes later, then give more hints, such as "Can the nail heads be held by two other nails?" The purpose is to facilitate proactive engagement within the groups. If no one can finish, upon consent of the participants, you should show them the answer and invite participants to try themselves. (Note: The 13 nails can be balanced on the head of one nail by arranging them as shown in Figure 1.) The participants will likely find the solution amazing and interesting, closing the gap between the participants.

4. Debriefing: Now is a good time to talk to the participants about what they found difficult about the task. Ask why they think the solution works.

5. Notes for the facilitator: This is a more complex game that can be used to enhance communication in small groups. Be sure to walk around to all of the groups. Encourage them to try different solutions. It is important to observe each participant in the small groups to see how they interact

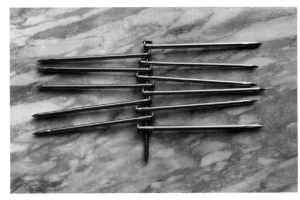
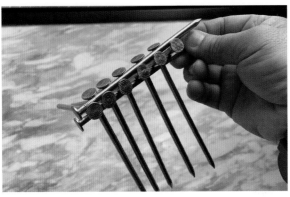

Figure 1: How to Balance the Nails

with each other. This will also provide important information to consider if other small groups are necessary in other games or activities.

Games without Tools

Example 1: Look and clap your hands

How to play:

The facilitator should stand with their arms stretched straight out in front of them with their hands facing each other. You will move both hands to face different directions so that the palms can be facing upward, downward, or towards each other. When the palms are facing each other, the group members should clap their hands once. The facilitator will repeat the movements, making fake moves from time to time or speeding up gradually. The game may conclude when the atmosphere reaches a climax. (For additional details, see Game 30 in Part II of this book.)

Facilitation and briefing:

1. Setting up and explaining the rules: Decide if you want the participants to be sitting or standing. Can they all see you? Explain how to play. It may be necessary to have a test round in which you change the positions of your hands. Move slowly to start and use exaggerated movements. Draw the group members' attention to the task and help increase their motivation.

2. Playing the game: The frequency and rhythm should be relatively slow at the beginning and then gradually increase. There will probably be some random clapping at the beginning, but this will stop as group members slowly find their order and rhythm with your hand movements. Smile! This is an important time to show group members your excitement about the game. They will feel this joy. This will also help them stay attentive. As the game gets faster, use signals from the group when it is reaching a climax — are group members

getting rowdy or losing attention? Is the whole group involved?

3. Debriefing: Discuss briefly if the group members feel more ready for the rest of the meeting or activities.

4. Notes for the facilitator: This kind of game can be used to ease into the meeting and other activities. It allows you to crack open personal comfort zones by providing a positive anchor (your hands) for relationship building. This is particularly important for groups of participants who have never met before. Observe each group member throughout the game. Are they clapping? Are they distracted? Are they energetic or subdued? Use these observations to inform your decisions about any subsequent games to use.

Example 2: Tapping fingers

How to play:

The facilitator should ask the group members to form a circle. Each member should then raise their left hand out to the left of their body with the palm open and facing forward. They should then place the index finger of their right hand on the open palm of the group member to their right. You should then explain that when you count down 3–2–1 (or, alternatively, you can use a specific word or movement they should respond to), they should close their left hand to try to tap or capture the finger of the member to the left and avoid being caught by the member to the right. (For other options, see Game 29 in Part II of this book.)

Facilitation and briefing:

1. Setting up and explaining the rules: It is important in this game to say one instruction and demonstrate each one at a time for group members to follow. It may also be necessary to help position the participants correctly if there is any confusion. Be sure to maintain eye contact with each group members in turn and instruct them how to make corresponding movements when appropriate.

2. Playing the game: It may take a few rounds for each person to get used to the rules. Once all participants appear to understand the movement, you can change the amount of time between each round.

3. Debriefing: This is a good time to create a sense of success for the entire group. You can start some discussion by asking: "Raise your hand if you caught someone's finger." This focuses on the positive aspect (rather than "raise your hand if your finger was caught", which focuses on the negative aspect). By identifying the positive side of the outcome, participants will be more eager to express themselves, while avoiding any embarrassment for anyone who was caught (and avoiding any awkward silence in response to the question). You should avoid using words like "lose", "win", "reward", and "penalty" for this game. Instead, use positive words to encourage participation and well-being, such as "please", "play the game", and "you've done it". The idea is to enhance the sense of success and happiness of the group members. Depending on the group dynamic, you can also consider requesting those who had their fingers caught to sing a song or to pick the next song the group will sing or listen to.

4. Notes for the facilitator: This game will increase physical contact and break barriers among group members. Be sure to observe each person to see how they are responding to this contact. You also have the option of moving people around to different positions in the circle during the game to help assist this. Check if there is anyone who seems to be struggling. While you may initially want to watch the participants play the game, once everyone is playing correctly, you should join them. You can also move between different group members, which will help you give a chance for each person to catch and be caught.

Conclusion

The information presented in this chapter can be summarised in a list of the eight essential skills for game facilitators. These were established previously by Dr Kin Sun Ng (unpublished).

1. Be open, be selfless, and enjoy yourself. Tap into your inner child.

2. Be confident and calm.

3. Know the number of participants and who they are in advance, including each participant's background, age, gender, and physical capabilities (e.g., able-bodied, physically disabled, mentally disabled, etc.).

4. Understand the venue, environment, equipment, table and chair arrangements, etc.

5. Avoid awkward silences:
    i. Face the participants and avoid turning away from them.
    ii. Avoid coerced participation, encourage voluntary participation.
    iii. Do not make fun of or scold participants who are not cooperating.

6. Research, innovate, evaluate, and improve.

7. Understand the timing and purpose of the game, and wrap up at the climax.

8. Be well prepared, explain clearly, practice in advance, and exaggerate the movements.

The example games presented in this chapter are broken down into the facilitation/briefing skills and considerations the facilitator should use to gain experience. The purpose of this is to get facilitators comfortable with running the games and to learn how to observe group members. These techniques can be further developed over time and tailored to each facilitator's personality. While the games listed in Part II of this book do not go into quite as much detailed analysis, many of the same considerations apply, and this chapter can be used as a reference for facilitators to analyse these aspects for each.

3

Debriefing Skills in Group Games

Kwok Wing Chan

Introduction

Debriefing is broadly defined as the facilitation of learning from experience (Greenaway, 2007a). The most noticeable example of this is when group members sit around to share their feelings and experience after a game. An "experience" is mainly composed of a series of activities with different goals and themes, while "learning" implies the application of knowledge to future tasks. The combined term "experiential learning" refers to the process in which group members are asked to reflect on, summarise, and transform their experiences to apply to future situations, thus allowing them to learn from their direct participation in the activities and experiences. Using this framework of experiential learning, this chapter uses relevant examples to explore the functions and timing for debriefing in group games. It goes on to introduce applicable debriefing models and methods, as well as common debriefing skills.

Functions of debriefing in group games

Debriefing is the process of using activity experience to promote self-learning, which gives meaning to the experience and brings out what can be learned from it through reflection, analysis, communication, and framing. It forms a close relationship with briefing and leading. Group games encourage participation and bring out themes of the meeting through game experience. These can be further elucidated during the debriefing. Almost all group games have elements of experiential learning, so including time for a game debriefing will enhance learning and create stronger bonds between the participants as well as between them and the facilitator.

Group game debriefing is usually integrated into the group development process, which not only helps transform and apply the experience learned from a group game to the group as a whole but also inspires group members to make personal and interpersonal discoveries. What group members discover and reflect on during a group game are often reflective of the group's characteristics and issues in general, and identifying various strengths and weaknesses can then assist and support group members in gradually applying what they have learned to daily life. Debriefing can also provide another space for participation and expression. It is a time for group members to observe and reflect, strengthen their observation abilities and sensibilities, and enhance their personal communication skills.

When to debrief during group games

Debriefing is generally scheduled for after the activity, but it can also be conducted before or in the early or middle stages of a game as a way to focus on previous experiences or consolidate the learning scenarios. Therefore, debriefing can be arranged before, during, or after a game as needed.

Before a game

Doing the debrief before the game is called "frontloading" (Priest & Gass, 1997), and it is intended to help group members go through what they learned from games in the past or their promised performances or actions. It is also a time to clarify the purpose and objectives of the game they are about to play and how they plan to learn by game experience. This process will heighten their interest and induce participation in addition to connecting the game with reality.

During a game

In most cases, the purpose of debriefing during a game is to deal with emergencies or make corrections and improvements in real time. The game needs to be paused for this kind of debriefing, which may disrupt the flow of the game. However, this intervention allows for quick shifts in focus or to bring the group members back to a common goal. For example, if a group activity needs to be suspended by the game facilitator because of repeated failures in a problem-solving game, it would be useful to ask the participants to take turns to explain their mood at that moment. Asking them what they need to do or what they need to avoid in order to succeed may also help them discover better practices.

After a game

The most common time to debrief is after a game is finished. The aim is to reflect on what participants have learned and experienced, which is the essence of debriefing. The length and depth of a debriefing session depend on the experience in the specific course of the game, the needs of group members, and the current progress of the group. Naturally, the type, complexity, and purpose of the game will also influence how much time is required to debrief. If each of these considerations is taken into account, a unique and illuminating debriefing may result from an activity that seems ordinary. However, it is also okay to shorten debriefing sessions if they are not helping the group achieve their purpose. This can be considered if you are receiving no responses or what seem to be standard or mechanical answers to your questions. The key is to understand the dynamics of the group and when it may be best to simply move on.

Experience-based debriefing models

Most experience-based debriefing models, including Borton's Three-stage Guided Model (Greenaway & Knapp, 2017; Priest & Gass, 1997; Schoel et al., 1988), Roger Greenaway's "4F" Poker Experience Reflection Method (Greenaway, 2007d, 2015), Priest and Gass's Funnel Method (Priest & Gass, 1997; Priest et al. 2000), and Thiagi's Six-stage Questioning Method (Thiagarajan & Thiagarajan, 1999), have been derived from Kolb's experiential learning cycle. Table 1 explains the basic structure and questioning procedures for these models. The following sections focus on introducing Kolb's experiential learning cycle and the "4F" poker experience reflection method.

Table 1: Experience-based Debriefing Models

Kolb Experiential Learning Cycle	Borton Three-stage Guided Model	Roger Greenaway "4F" Poker Experience Reflection Method	Priest & Gass Funnel Method	Thiagi Six-stage Questioning Method
Concrete Experience				
Reflective Observation	What?	Facts	Review	How did you feel?
		Feeling	Recall and Remember	
Abstract Conceptualisation	So what?	Finding	Affect and Effect	What did you learn?
			Summation	How did it relate?
				What if?
Active Experimentation	Now what?	Future	Application	What next?
			Commitment	

Experiential Learning Cycle

The experiential learning cycle proposed by Kolb is the basis of the above debriefing models and consists of the following four consecutive stages (Beard & Wilson, 2002; Nadler & Luckner, 1997; Priest & Gass, 1997).

1. Concrete experience: The first stage of the learning cycle is the group members' experience of the activities, including the series of planned games or challenging activities.

2. Reflective observation: Reflection can be understood as the time group members take to step back to re-observe and review their experience, with the aims of getting additional insight into how they feel about the activities (as well as what they have seen and heard during the process) and connecting these insights with relevant past experience.

3. Abstract conceptualisation: In this stage, the group members summarise their reflections and develop them into knowledge concepts, including identifying learning methods, problem-solving skills, and effective group participative behaviours from their experience. This is also a time to make discoveries in their personal understanding, emotions, and behaviour pattern, etc., for application in similar circumstances in future.

4. Active experimentation: This stage focuses on applying the experiences summarised to similar circumstances or daily life. We can apply such methods as changing actions, learning to plan, committing to improve, or developing plans for action.

"4F" Poker Experience Reflection Method

It is easy to master the "4F" poker experience reflection method proposed by Roger Greenaway. This method involves comprehensive and interesting perspectives for asking questions. "4F" represents the four courses of reflection: facts, feelings, findings, and future. These correspond to the four poker suits — diamonds, hearts, spades, and clubs, respectively — which are helpful identifiers for understanding and applying this model (Greenaway, 2007d).

Diamonds, corresponding to facts, represent the situation and impressions presented by the experience for the first time. Relevant questions a facilitator can ask when using this model of debriefing are: What did we see and hear just now? What was the most unforgettable, different, or interesting?

Hearts, corresponding to feelings, are designed for discussion of the emotions, feelings, and intuitions evoked during the game. Common questions include: What were your deepest feelings during the game? When did you feel you were the most or the least immersed? How does this compare to your feelings during other games or your previous experiences?

Spades, representing findings, take the meaning of "shovel" to symbolise excavation. Questions related to this could include: What did we learn? What did we find?

Clubs, corresponding to future, represent the actions of learning transfer and change as well as growth in the future. This discussion can include action plans, learning plans, choices, drills, and even dreams. Relevant questions include: What will you stop doing, begin doing, or continue to do? What do you want to get from the experience? How can we apply what we learned in the future?

The joker card is also given significance in this model. It represents a "wild card" that can be used flexibly. It is meant to act as a reminder not to rigidly turn what should be a "reflection course" into a mechanical and orderly "4F course". Instead, the proper order of these reflections and depth should be based on the experience and attitude of the group members.

Debriefing skills

The following sections detail various debriefing skills, ranging from the basic principles to questioning skills and techniques for inviting participants to speak.

Basic principles

The basic principles of debriefing and guided group discussion have been outlined in numerous sources (Doherty et al., 2000; Priest & Gass, 1997; Priest et al., 2000). These principles are summarised below based on a person's role as a participant or facilitator.

As a participant:

1. Ensure that everyone participates.

2. Only one person speaks at a time. Avoid interrupting others.

3. Allow other group members not to answer questions if they do not want to.

4. Observe the confidentiality principle.

As a facilitator:

1. Ask open questions.

2. Allow adequate and suitable pauses. Avoid speaking too fast.

3. Listen carefully and clarify the feelings and content you want to focus on via paraphrasing.

4. Appreciate and recognise the contributions of each group member and express this with appropriate body language and words.

5. Encourage group members to express things in their own way without interrupting with suggestions for expressions or words. Try not to complete their unfinished thoughts or clarify their ideas for the group. Instead, let them speak and ask for clarification if something is confusing. This will help the reflection to better represent the group members' collective values and demands.

6. Help and lead group members to face their struggles with personal expression and help turn difficulties into opportunities for study.

7. Actively guide group members to find answers to their problems by questioning rather than directly giving a solution.

8. Encourage group members to conduct self-evaluations instead of comparing and criticising them.

9. Guide group members to express their opinions, ideas, feelings, and intentions rather than give speeches or exhortations.

10. Prepare relevant guiding questions or debriefing activities, whose adoption should be

determined based on the group atmosphere, dynamic, and collective experience.

11. Discuss positive aspects (strengths and successes) before dealing with negative aspects (defects and failures).

12. Give priority to events and topics related to safety and trust.

13. Decide on the timing and duration for discussion in line with the stages of group development and demands of group members. Postpone the discussion when group members need to take a break.

Questioning skills

Debriefing skills are developed based on questioning, and common debriefing models are also, therefore, constituted based on a specific series of questions. Debriefing and questioning should match the contents and themes of the game as well as group development, objectives, etc. The relationship-oriented and success-oriented questioning models, described below, are two examples of questioning skills a facilitator should develop.

Relationship-oriented questioning

This model focuses on questions relating to "who", such as "who knows?", "who is similar?", "who knows the best?", and "who first finds?" Relationship-oriented questioning aims to improve group cohesion, build a sense of identity, and enhance interpersonal learning abilities of group members via their relationship. At the initial stage of group development, the use of "we" in the discussion is essential to strengthen collective awareness. After the group develops, more emphasis can be put on individuals to promote personal reflection and transformation.

Success-oriented questioning

With the aim of exploring positive experience, success-oriented questioning recognises the abilities of group members based on what has been successful, what strengths they possess,

or what has been achieved (Greenaway, 2007c). There are three ways of questioning. The first is to start the discussion after the abilities of group members have been recognised based on positive aspects, advantages, and strengths which were apparent during the game. This will then allow the group to transform defects into objectives and actions for improvement. The second way of questioning is to seek exceptions in negative, failed, and problematic aspects, and then explore and recognise the abilities of group members through discussion over the exceptions to these issues. The third is to take the approach of "rating". For example, if a group member rates a problem during a game at 8 on a scale of 1–10 (1 being the best and 10 being the worst), then the facilitator can ask questions about how they came to this conclusion. What do the two points between 8 and 10 represent? Group members can then be guided to discuss the efforts they made that prevented the situation from being worse. What could have been done to shift this to a better score? Do the group members all agree with that rating? If another group member rates the issue differently, then this is also an opportunity to ask questions to highlight the different experiences during the game.

Techniques for inviting participants to speak

One key aspect of group discussion and debriefing that must be adhered to is speaking in turns. Each group member deserves time to speak and be heard. To avoid interruptions or speaking all at once, facilitators can utilise specific techniques, such as speaking in turn, going into and out of the circle, 1–2–all, and scaling.

Speak in turn (round)

Speaking in turn is the most commonly used debriefing technique to open up a conversation, focus on a topic, guide silent group members to speak, and motivate participation of the entire group (Harvill et al., 2011). Speaking in turn may start with a topic such as "take turns to tell everyone what impressed you most in the game" or with an adjective such as "take turns to describe your feelings about the game in one word". Participants can also be prompted to finish statements such as "I like it when I ...".

When using this technique, the facilitator should give the group members a silent period (usually 10 seconds to 1 minute) to prepare what they want to say. It is important that during each participant's turn to speak, none of the other group members (or the facilitator) should interrupt. The facilitator may change the order in which the group members speak from time to time (i.e., start a round of speeches clockwise or counter clockwise or try to arrange a silent group member to speak in the middle).

Going into and out of the circle

This technique requires the group to use a rope to form a circle of appropriate size. Everyone should start standing outside the circle to show a clear boundary between inside and outside. The facilitator can then ask the group members to recall a certain discovery or experience they had during the game, such as "describe a merit you saw in yourself", "describe a moment when you helped others or the group as a whole", "describe a moment in the game you enjoyed", etc. The group members will then move under the rope and into the circle when they freely share their views on the topic one by one. This movement of leaving the group to enter the circle represents the process of personal reflection, and the questions or speaking prompts should reflect this.

When that round of speeches ends and everyone is in the circle, the facilitator will raise another topic which is similar in action but of a different level, such as "what did you appreciate the most about the group", "describe an occasion where the group or a group member helped you", and "what do you like best about the group". This time, in a similar manner as the first round, the facilitator will tell the members to first go out of the circle and then speak until all members go back to their original place. This movement of leaving the circle to form a group represents inclusiveness and supports the formation of the group.

The facilitator should also consider initiating another round by having group members refer to

contributions by another member as they exit the circle, then that member would exit the circle and refer to the contribution of another member, and so on, until all of the participants are outside the circle. The use of this version of the technique should be reserved for groups that are familiar with each other so there is no confusion about any names.

1-2-all

In this technique, established by Greenaway (2007b), "1" stands for the time spent in thinking, reflection, sentence-making, or recording; "2" refers to the time for dyad group sharing, discussion, or interviews; and "all" indicates the time for discussion or reporting at the level of the whole group. For example, the facilitator can ask that participants take half a minute to remember the most profound experience of the game, and then request that they share their thoughts and contributions to the game with one partner. After these dyad groups are allowed to discuss briefly, everyone can return to the main group to report and discuss their experiences.

Scaling

"Rating" is the process of placing subjective ideas, feelings, attitudes, and opinions into pre-set criterion for communication and comparison. It is often used to understand perspectives, to focus on issues, and to review the target objectives (Greenaway, 2002). Relevant examples of facilitator prompts for discussion include the following.

1. Verbal energy rating: Ask that participants use a scale of 1 to 10 to express their current participation energy (1 for listless and 10 for exuberant). Then discuss why they feel that way and what could mediate positive change in their rating.

2. Visual mood rating: Ask group members to show your present mood by gesture. Tell them to (a) raise a hand straight up and keep their palm flat if they are excited and happy; (b) put their hands in front of their waist if

they are in a bad mood and lack motivation; and (c) put their hands flat over their mouth if they are in a calm or neutral mood.

3. Visual rating of participation: Ask group members to stand in a circle and think about the activity just completed. Then request them to step to a position inside the circle based on their contribution to the game. Explain that the greater their contribution was, the closer they should stand to the centre of the group circle. Thus, small or ordinary contributors should stand a few step into the middle of the circle from their current position; moderate contributions should move forward a few steps towards the centre; and large contributions should move into the centre of the circle. Once people are standing where they think they should be, ask each person to explain why they are at that level. (This can also be done using two parallel lines with space between to accommodate the varying levels. Participants can move from one line towards the other based on what they perceived their contribution to be.)

Regardless of the style used, the purpose of the scaling technique is not only to measure the result itself and encourage self-reflection, but also to establish a visual representation to help solidify each participant's understanding of their position for each theme. Such reference points will help group members view themselves within the group and provide a moment for them to give explanations and reasons for their rating, as well as time for the group to establish goals and actions to be successful.

Conclusion

In conclusion, the group members' value orientation is the most important aspect to consider in the practice of debriefing in group games. The facilitator's responsibility is not to preach or teach but to guide the group members to summarise and achieve transformation and apply what they have learned. The ultimate goal is to help the group members know how to effectively debrief after an event, be it a game or a life experience. The self-reflection and learning abilities of the group members are gradually improved thanks to the demonstration, explanation, and self-debriefing activities arranged for the group and through the participation of other members as well as the facilitator in these processes.

References

Beard, C., & Wilson, J.P. (2002). *The power of experiential learning: A handbook for trainers and educators*. Kogan Page.

Doherty, D.A., Garvey, K.L., Gass, M., & Sugerman, D.A. (2000). *Reflective learning: Theory and practice*. Kendall/Hunt.

Greenaway, R. (1993). *Playback: A guide to reviewing activities*. The Duke of Edinburgh's Award published in association with Endeavour Scotland.

Greenaway, R. (2002). *Reviewing with ropes*. The Active Reviewing Guide website. http://reviewing.co.uk/articles/ropes.htm.

Greenaway, R. (2007a). Dynamic reviewing. In M.L. Silberman (Ed.), *The handbook of experiential learning* (pp. 59–80). Pfeiffer.

Greenaway, R. (2007b). *Reviewing for all: How to include everyone in a lively debrief*. The Active Reviewing Guide website. https://reviewing.co.uk/archives/art/9_2.htm.

Greenaway, R. (2007c). *Reviewing success*. The Active Reviewing Guide website. https://reviewing.co.uk/success/index.htm.

Greenaway, R. (2007d). *The active reviewing cycle*. The Active Reviewing Guide website. http://reviewing.co.uk/learning-cycle/index.htm.

Greenaway, R., & Knapp, C.E. (2017). Reviewing and reflection: Connecting people to experience. In B. Humberstone, P. Heater, & K.A. Henderson (Eds.), *Routledge international handbook of outdoor studies* (pp. 260–268). Routledge.

Greenaway, R., Vaida, B., & Iepure, C. (2015). *Active reviewing: A practical guide for trainers and facilitators* [Kindle DX version]. https://activereviewing.com.

Harvill, R.L., Jacobs, E.J., Masson, R.L., & Schimmel, C.J. (2011). *Group counselling: Strategies and skills* (7th ed.). Cengage Learning.

Nadler, R., & Luckner, J.L. (1997). *Processing the experience: Strategies to enhance and generalize learning* (2nd ed.). Kendall/Hunt.

Priest, S., & Gass, M. (1997). *Effective leadership in adventure programming*. Human Kinetics.

Priest, S., Gass, M., & Gillis, L. (2000). *The essential elements of facilitation*. Kendall/Hunt.

Schoel, J., Prouty, D., & Radcliffe, P. (1988). *Island of healing: A guide to adventure based counselling*. Project Adventure.

Thiagarajan, S., & Thiagarajan, R. (1999). *Facilitator's toolkit*. Workshops by Thiagi.

Risk Assessment and Prevention when Leading Group Games

Fai Kuen Leung

Introduction

According to various accident statistics and reports from Project Adventure Inc. (1971), in the United States, activities with the highest injury rates are not rock climbing, high event challenge courses, abseiling, or seemingly more hazardous activities, but initiative games, which are commonly used by social workers. Though this study was conducted in 1971, it is still the most commonly cited source for such statistics (e.g., in Godsey, 2005). Below are some possible causes of such accidents during group games, according to a mountaineering safety manual published by the New Zealand Mountain Safety Council (Cathye, 1993).

1. Failure to observe carefully, hence underestimating the risk of accidents. Such oversight may involve the environment, use of facilities, equipment or errors in execution, such as picking a dangerous location.

2. Dangerous moves made by group members and facilitators. Accidents related to this can stem from facilitators overestimating the group members' abilities or when group members do not understand the rules fully or simply make excessive movements during a game.

3. Inadequate awareness of the game's potential hazards by the facilitator, who may have also overestimated themselves with regard to their ability to host a particular game. Certain activities are inherently hazardous to some degree. Yet facilitators may attempt to lead such activities without enough practice. They are ill-prepared to foresee the safety and hazardous aspects of the activities, which can easily lead to accidents.

With such accidents being possible, it is essential to understand the risks and how to prevent mishaps when leading group games. This chapter outlines some accident statistics and the classification of risks, as well as methods of risk assessment and accident prevention in group games. These theories are then demonstrated with cases relevant to social service organisations and educational institutions.

The iceberg of risks (the 1:10:30:600 ratio)

Figure 2 illustrates that for every single fatal accident (shown at the tip of the iceberg), there are 10 cases of physical trauma, 30 cases of physical injuries, and 600 near misses where accidents almost occurred during games and activities. Thus, although severe injuries and fatalities often receive more attention, an even higher number of people have suffered because of poor safety awareness and standards (Cathye, 1993). These data are a reminder that near misses without obvious wounds or injuries are not uncommon in group games. When safety is disregarded or risks are not assessed fully and prevented, serious accidents can occur with a range of consequences.

Concepts and methods of risk assessment

To prevent unnecessary danger, each game must be evaluated before taking place. This assessment should consider five major interconnected

aspects: people, facilitator, activity, facilities and equipment, and surrounding environment. However, it is important to understand that accidents are typically not caused by one single event or triggered by just one of these factors, but they are often the result of a combination of issues or a chain of multiple errors that bring about a series of consequences. This is illustrated in Figure 3.

The following sections discuss specific points the facilitator must understand about each aspect in order to fully appreciate the risk level for each game.

People

This category is focused on who the group members are. Group composition can vary widely depending on the situation and might include children, teenagers, adults, elderly, students, lead teachers, lead social workers, other facilitators, or other supporting personnel. The abilities of each participant as well as the group as a whole must be included in the assessment. Their abilities can be evaluated in terms of their:

1. Physical fitness—not limited to the fitness required to overcome wild terrain but also needs to consider the body movements required for the game as well as the group members' personal injuries and sicknesses;

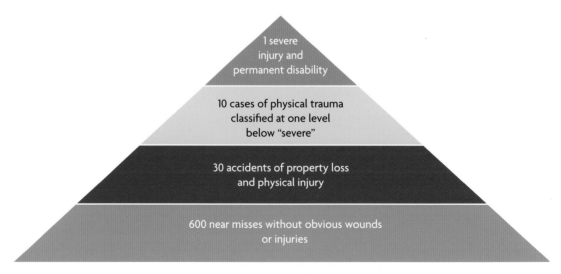

Figure 2: Iceberg of Risks

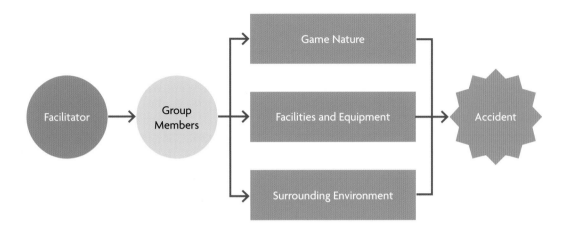

Figure 3: Flow of Errors that Can Contribute to Accidents during a Group Game

2. State of health — however, this does not mean excluding everyone with a chronic illness or obvious health issues so long as they have been proven fit for participation in a pre-activity medical check and the planned activity is suitable or they have a special caretaker to assist them;

3. Ability and skills — group members will struggle in a game that is too technically demanding, but they may also get bored if the skill level falls too low, so it is essential that the facilitator is able to shift the level of difficulty up and down based on their observations of the group members as well as help manage any overly confident group members who are prone to injuries; and

4. Psychological and mental state — while physical conditions and limitations are often relatively easy to spot, a participant's psychological and mental state will require keen observation by the facilitator before and during a game to detect when group members are under stress from lack of sleep, for example.

It is important for the facilitator to also understand why the participants have come together and what their relationship is with the rest of the group as this will also affect their individual abilities and health. For instance, when a facilitator is running a game at a training camp, they will need to consider the rest of the training the participants are undergoing which will affect their physical, mental, and emotional health. Some training schedules are jam-packed from dawn to dusk, or even have group members wake in the middle of the night, as a way to help them push their physical and mental limits during stress. However, participants may begin to fall apart when they get too exhausted, exposing other hidden health problems. Furthermore, some illnesses may seem physiological but can be triggered by psychological factors, including depression, hypertension, diabetes, heart disease, epilepsy, and so on. It is therefore important to know whether any or all group members participating in the game are suffering from such illnesses or are under identifiable stress. Some of this information can be gathered in advance of the game, but at other times, the facilitator may need to make a snap assessment (and possibly change the game choice or level of difficulty) based on what they observe immediately before or during the game.

Facilitator

The first three chapters of this book detail the skills a facilitator should possess and the steps they should follow to host successful games. However, in addition to these skills, the facilitator should also assess their own health and fitness based on the same categories listed above. As the facilitator should also be playing the game in addition to demonstrating it to the participants, they need to ensure that they choose games they can perform the movements for. This requires practicing the games and intimately understanding the changes in difficulty for each. In some cases, particularly for games requiring climbing, bouncing, or falling (such as "The High Wall" and "Trust Fall"), a professional instructor should be asked to help lead the participants and facilitator when playing the game. This will help mitigate any undue risks of accidents.

Activity

The design of each activity or game is directly related to the inherent level of risk involved. There are three primary factors to consider when assessing the game to be played.

1. Physical risks—the physical abilities required for a game are often clearly outlined in the rules or explanation of how to play. The physical risks of a game may be higher when playing with group members who are prone to injuries or have physical limitations. The physical risks of a game also involve the surroundings and facilities, discussed further below. The timing of a game may also introduce unnecessary risk, such as playing a more physical game without any warm-up or stretching. Games and sequences of games should be designed based on these physical risks.

2. Psychological risks—some games involve competition or require a certain level of competence. Some group members may be unable to cope with high-stress situations (such as timed activities) or competition. Being unable to complete tasks may also cause shame or embarrassment. Certain games which link the lack of results with a "punishment" can also increase the risk of participants having emotional or psychological breakdowns. Accidents not only include situations resulting in physical injury but also negative mental and emotional "injuries" (which can have subsequent physical consequences). The decision to play a game with a certain group of participants must consider these risks.

3. Team objective risks—games are played with a specific objective in mind for that group of participants. Facilitators should harness team spirit with care, focusing only on positive and supportive encouragement to move the group towards their defined objective. Using misapplied pressure to force group members to complete the game or creating unnecessary competitive tension can undermine the purpose of the gathering. Failure to achieve the desired objective can also result in physical and psychological risks for participants.

Facilities and equipment

The facilities and equipment have a significant role in determining the level of danger when playing a game. While these risks tend to correspond to physical consequences, they can also affect the mental well-being and feelings of safety for participants. Facilitators should consider the following three aspects to ensure that such risks are minimised.

1. Be familiar with the operation of related facilities and equipment—many facilitators use facilities for dangerous activities without prior training. The difference between a trained and untrained facilitator lies in their awareness of hazard prevention, means of intervention when hazards occur, and how capable they are in guiding group members to help deal with the current hazards. Facilitators need to be aware of their own limitations and request help and guidance when necessary. They should obtain any requisite certifications and repeatedly practice using the facilities and equipment themselves before hosting the game with participants.

2. Use the proper equipment designated for each game—each game requires different tools or equipment. If these tools or equipment are not accessible, then the facilitator should not attempt to use other unsuitable equipment. This can be determined prior to playing the games during an inspection of the facilities and equipment. The facilitator is typically responsible for providing the tools and

equipment necessary for the game and should make sure to book these in advance. If tools or equipment must be substituted in a game, then the facilitator must test these substitutes well before to determine their suitability. This will naturally be easier for games requiring low-risk tools (such as substituting a different stuffed toy for the rubber chicken mentioned in the example game "Chicken thrower" in Chapter 3) than it will be for high-risk activities (such as substituting the platform for "Trust Fall" with a ledge set at a different height). If the facilitator is unfamiliar with the facilities or equipment required for a game, then they should consider requesting assistance from a professional instructor.

3. Ensure facilities and equipment are well maintained and meet international and local standards—the standards and maintenance schedule for facilities and equipment will depend on the activity. While this may be conducted by the facility owners, it is up to the game facilitator to ensure that the facilities and equipment follow these standards before conducting the activity. Some equipment standards will be more stringent than others and may vary by country. In the case of the "Trust Fall", for example, the standard height for the platforms in the United States is five feet high, while the standard height for platforms in Hong Kong is set at three and a half to four feet. These standards reflect the difference in average height of Americans and Chinese people. Similarly, the standards for the equipment and facilities for adventure games are often set based on guidelines in the United States, so it may be necessary for facilitators to vet these standards before conducting the activities in other regions. Following standards blindly without thinking or using facilities or equipment that are not well-maintained will only lead to accidents. Again, if the facilitator is unfamiliar with the standards required for the facilities or equipment needed for a game, then they should request help from a professional instructor.

Surrounding environment

Along with the facilities and equipment required for a game, the surrounding environment will play a significant role in the level of physical and mental risks for group members participating in an activity. There are four things facilitators should do to assess and minimise these risks.

1. Arrange to visit the activity venue—the venue for a game should be carefully vetted to ensure it is the most suitable option. For example, a barbecue area is not appropriate for a game requiring space to run around. Such visits should involve checking the facilities and equipment (as outlined above) as well as the site logistics to ensure a smooth transition between activities. These visits should also include checking the toilet and hygiene facilities as well as areas to sleep (if the activities will be conducted over multiple days). It is also important to assess contingency plans in case of accidents or emergencies, especially if you are in a remote rural area.

2. Determine the need for permits or notifying authorities—this may apply if you are hosting activities in country parks or campgrounds as well as if you are conducting games that require certain equipment (such as adventure games involving tree climbing or rope ladders or swinging). Not obtaining the proper permission or permits may result in fees, penalties, or persecution. Even smaller venues, like conference rooms or gymnasiums, often require booking in advance and liability waivers to be signed. Facilitators must be familiar with such prerequisites before organising an activity.

3. Being aware of the local weather and have a backup plan—this is particularly important when hosting games outside. The facilitator should assess how the weather could affect the venue and the participants. For example, be aware of any areas prone to flooding or flash floods, cliff edge erosion, shaded areas versus full sun exposure, muddy areas, etc. A contingency plan should be established based on where participants can seek shelter

if necessary as well as different games that can be played to achieve the same objectives when the weather prevents the original game from being played.

4. Arrange pre-activity field trips with participants—optional field trips to view the locations with all or some of the participants can be an excellent way to gauge their perceived comfort levels. This will be particularly important for groups that have physical or psychological limitations. Allowing participants to get familiar with the site's logistics will go a long way to increase their confidence and feelings of safety as well as ensuring a smooth transition between activities.

Risk classification based on activity nature

After assessing the five components contributing to the risk level of a game, the actual risk of the game (low to high) can be compared with the level of risk awareness (low to high) of the facilitator and participants. This results in a four quadrant classification (Figure 4). The four classifications are: danger zone (extreme risk), match-high (peak

experience), match-low (explore and understand), and danger zone (psychological, traumatic).

Danger zone (extreme risk)

Low personal risk awareness coupled with high actual risk corresponds to situations in the danger zone (extreme risk) category. Such situations will likely involve neglected safety techniques and lead to accidents. Serious accidents are often compounded because the facilitator will be incapable of dealing with the accident once it has occurred. Examples of games that may fall into this category if the facilitator's awareness is insufficient include "The High Wall", "Low Beam", "Trust Fall", and "Confidence Leap".

Match-high (peak experience)

Generally speaking, when the risk awareness matches the actual risk level, appropriate safety techniques would be adopted by the facilitator and the participants to exercise caution. For example, when participants are well-versed in the possible risks and the facilitator has received relevant training and can deal with high risk games, such as those listed in the category above, then

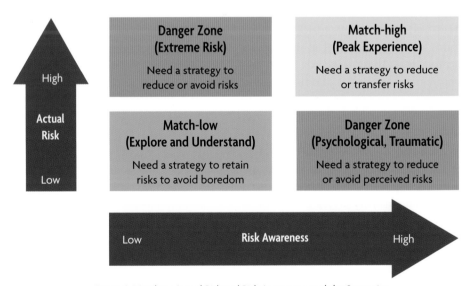

Figure 4: Matching Actual Risk and Risk Awareness, and the Strategies to Manage Them (adapted from Ewert, 1989).

the objectives of the games can be successfully achieved in a safe and fun manner.

Match-low (explore and understand)

When the risk and awareness are both low, the probability of an accident occurring is relatively low. However, facilitators should not be complacent and should incorporate diverse elements or increase the level of difficulty in the game to prevent participants from taking risky actions out of boredom.

Danger zone (psychological, traumatic)

When the actual risk is low but the perceived risks in terms of awareness is high, group members can experience unnecessary psychological pressure and trauma during an activity. Such situations can arise from a participant feeling too much peer pressure to play a game that makes them uncomfortable, even when the game is considered low-risk. Understanding the backgrounds and limitations of each group member as well as observing their behaviour during the activities will allow the facilitator to make informed decisions about what games to play to avoid falling into this category.

Strategies to address risks

Addressing risks involves a decision-making process, which requires the formulation of an appropriate risk response strategy based on the actual and perceived risks of the activity, the facilitator's capabilities, and the participants' awareness and adherence to the safety rules. The following is a brief introduction to four risk management strategies and the risk classifications they apply to.

1. Retain risks — this strategy involves maintaining the current level of risk or even adding some difficulty or complexity to the game and would be adopted when the frequency and severity of accidents are low upon assessment. Applicable to the match-low (explore and understand) risk classification.

2. Reduce risks — reducing the hazard level by substitution or other means can be accomplished using several strategies, including:

   i. Enforce proper rules and safety guidelines (for example, the game facilitator in Hong Kong needs to ensure a facilitator to participant ratio of 1:16 for low event challenge activities, as stipulated by The Challenge Course Association of Hong Kong, China);

   ii. Adopt proper game facilitation and leading styles;

   iii. Know the group members in advance, understand their physical, mental, and psychological limitations and strengths;

   iv. Use step-by-step teaching according to the competencies of group members;

   v. Teach group members safety techniques and promote safety awareness; and

   vi. Explain the risk level of each activity to the group members before playing the game.

   Applicable to the danger zone (extreme risk) and danger zone (psychological, traumatic) risk classifications as well as match-high (peak experience), in some cases.

3. Avoid risks — this strategy should be considered when despite every effort made to control and manage the related risks, the accidents arising during the game have been so serious and frequent that the facilitator has determined it is better to adopt avoidance strategies. This risk management strategy applies to the danger zone (extreme risk) and danger zone (psychological, traumatic) risk classifications.

4. Transfer risks — a commonly adopted strategy in which a facilitator will engage a professional to lead the activity, or enable the group members to make a fully informed decision on whether to continue the activity, while knowing that they have to bear the necessary responsibilities. This risk management strategy applies to the match-high (peak experience) risk classification.

Duty of care

Game facilitators have a duty to ensure the safety of participants and must make this a serious priority (Scannell & Scannell, 2010). If an accident does occur and results in a participant being injured, the facilitator is likely to bear the legal responsibilities, particularly if the event was caused by the facilitator's negligence or lack of awareness. Matching suitably challenging activities with the abilities of the participants requires experience and keen observation skills. The risks and benefits must be carefully balanced and assessed. It is also the facilitator's responsibility to keep the participants safe from any potential dangers in the environment. If ever in doubt, facilitators are advised to refer to the risk assessment guidelines or the best practices manual on safety precautions in their country or region and consult law professionals for legal advice regarding their duty of care.

Conclusion

Games empower group members to learn and grow individually as well as develop interpersonal relationships with others. This is made possible first and foremost by the group facilitator's efforts, including prior risk assessment, proper intervention in the course of the games, and paying attention to the group members' personal growth. However, an accident will deal a big blow to these efforts. The above risk management strategies not only aim to prevent physical injury to the group members but also seek to avoid psychological trauma. Therefore, when leading a group game, facilitators should follow these steps.

1. Evaluate the surroundings and equipment necessary for the game to determine their suitability and safety. For instance, games involving running must take place in an open area, while the venue for a blindfold game cannot have too many obstacles.

2. Determine and practice the body movements required for each game and identify any potential hazards. In blindfold games, for example, design protective moves for group members as they might bump into each other.

3. In games identified to be higher risk, participants should be instructed how to observe the safety rules more prudently. However, a balance should be struck between enforcing the safety rules and ensuring that the game is still fun for the participants.

4. Teach group members how to protect themselves and avoid accidents before conducting a game that involves particularly dangerous actions.

5. In the course of each game, carefully observe and try to predict the actions of group members in order to prevent them from making dangerous moves.

6. Observe the duty of care principle at all stages of the game to ensure that safety is a priority. Consider the abilities of participants for dealing with the challenges of certain games and take care to keep them safe from both physical and psychological harm.

References

Cathye, H. (1993). *Managing risks in outdoor activities: Mountain safety manual*. New Zealand Mountain Safety Council.

Ewert, A. (1989). *Outdoor adventure pursuits: Foundations, models and theories*. Publishing Horizons.

Project Adventure Inc. (1971). *A 20 Year Safety Study*.

Godsey, J. (2005). *Challenge course safety: A study of manageable factors contributing to incidents on high elements*. University of Oklahoma Norman.

Scannell, M., & Scannell, E.E. (2010). *The big book of team motivation games*. McGraw-Hill.

Part II
100 Group Games

Introduction and Game Structure

The following section describes 100 different games that can be played with groups of varying sizes and experience. They are divided into four categories: warm-up and ice-breaking games, mutual understanding games, group cooperation and cohesion games, and problem-solving games.

Each game includes general information about how long the game takes to play, the number of participants needed, and a list of any required materials. Some games require even numbers of group members. In situations with an odd number of participants, some group members can be asked to act as judges with the game facilitator. Alternatively, if there is no need for a judge to monitor the game, then the game facilitator can also play so there are even teams. The next section for each game explains the objective(s) of the game, followed by the steps and procedures for how to play the game. Each game concludes with some reminders and precautions the facilitator should be aware of as well as any debriefing required. The game facilitator can use the information presented in these sections to develop a list of rules they should explain to the group members. The level of detail they should include will vary based on the age and experience of the participants. Images are included to help demonstrate a game when necessary.

As the previous chapters explain, it is important for a game facilitator to understand the purpose for playing a game to ensure that this matches the objective(s) of the game being played. Thus, some of the games are explained in vague terms for a general understanding, leaving the details to be decided by the game facilitator. They should also be creative with how each game is used and can improvise the rules to keep the game exciting for all of the participants. Many of the games can also be altered to avoid physical contact between group members or can be played over video conferencing (e.g., Zoom, Skype, etc.).

1

Warm-up and
Ice-breaking Games

1

 10 minutes

 At least 10
(if there are more
than 10 participants,
then two participants
will have to be
superheroes)

 None

Reminders and precautions

1. When the superhero is found, the facilitator should focus on the safety of all group members and help them avoid injury as they race to line up and touch the shoulders of the person in front of them.

2. The game facilitator may need to lead the superhero to an open space to give the group members space to line up.

3. This game may not be appropriate for group members with impaired hearing or vision.

4. This game needs to be carried out in a room or on flat ground without obstacles.

Debriefing

None.

I am a superhero

Objectives

Allow group members to move around and meet different people as well as to create a relaxed atmosphere.

How to play

1. Ask group members to form a circle and then to close their eyes.

2. The game facilitator will then walk around behind the circle and lightly touch or tap one of the group members on the shoulder (if the number of the participants is large, then the game facilitator may tap two group members). This member will become the superhero.

3. All of the group members should then open their eyes and move around to ask other members "Are you the superhero?" If the member is not the superhero, then they need to respond "I am not the superhero!" They should also shake or wave their hands around.

4. The superhero (the touched member) cannot admit that they are the superhero during the first, second, or third time of being asked. When they are asked for the fourth time, they would have to raise their hand and shout "I am the superhero!"

5. When the superhero is found, all group members must line up behind the superhero as fast as possible and touch the shoulders of the person in front of them. If there are two superheroes in the group and they raise their hands simultaneously, then the group members can make two different lines.

6. The game can be modified by changing the language of the question and answer to a messy or self-created language. The identity can also be changed from a superhero to any other quality, such as "I am a hardworking person".

Group members should ask other members "Are you the superhero?"

When the superhero is asked for the fourth time, they should raise their hand and shout "I am the superhero!" All group members must then line up behind the superhero as fast as possible and touch the shoulders of the person in front of them.

2

 15 minutes

 No limit

 None

Loud and low voices

Objectives

Help the members warm-up and provide them with opportunities to speak up and cooperate with each other.

How to play

1. Invite a group member ("A") to leave the room for a moment.

2. The game facilitator should then help or allow other members to decide on a category (e.g., fruits, flowers, countries, etc.).

3. Once decided, Member A should come back into the room.

4. Member A may choose either a loud or low voice.

5. Upon choosing, the other members need to follow the selected tone of voice in saying different kinds of the selected category simultaneously (e.g., if the category is fruits, then each member would say the name of a fruit like orange, banana, apple, and so on).

6. If Member A can correctly guess the category, then they win.

7. To increase difficulty, the game facilitator may set a limit to the number of guesses Member A has to guess the category.

Reminders and precautions

This game is not suitable for playing at night as the "loud voices" option may cause a disturbance.

Debriefing

Help members understand that Member A may not easily guess the correct answer if all other members operate collectively and cooperatively.

3

 20 minutes

 No limit

 None

Random game

Objectives

Make the group members feel engaged and happy as well as increase interaction between them.

How to play

1. The game facilitator should demonstrate how to play the game first. For example, they can say "This is yellow" while pointing to a yellow door, or "This is red" while pointing to a member in red clothes.

2. Then the facilitator should ask all the group members to roam around to find things and then say the colour of that thing. For example, the floor, chair, door, lamp, or a member's clothing and accessories.

3. After saying the colour, the group members can point to an object and say the object.

4. Group members may also point to a person and say the name of that person.

5. When the game ends, the facilitator may praise the group members for doing a great job.

Reminders and precautions

This game is not suitable for colour-blind people.

Debriefing

None.

4

 20 minutes

 No limit

 None

Cattle across the mountain

Objectives

Provide members with a chance to speak loudly and interact with each other to create a relaxing atmosphere.

How to play

1. Group members should be equally divided into two teams; one team is the "mountain team" and the other is the "cattle team".

2. Members of each team should stand side by side, facing the members of the other team. The cattle team members should kneel to imitate cattle.

3. The cattle team selects one representative to stand at the back of the mountain team. The mountain team needs to privately choose one cattle team member and then tell the representative of the cattle team the name of their chosen member, without letting the other cattle team members know.

4. When the game starts, the representative of the cattle team will shout out the name of the selected team member. Simultaneously, the members of the mountain team will arbitrarily shout together, preventing the cattle team from hearing or guessing the correct name.

5. The cattle team wins if they can correctly state the name; otherwise, their representative will become a member of the mountain team.

6. The two teams will swap roles and continue the game.

7. The game can be played for a set amount of time or until one team reaches a certain number of members.

Reminders and precautions

1. This game is not suitable to be played at night as it requires yelling and loud noises.
2. This game is recommended to be played in an open area where others will not be disturbed.

Debriefing

None.

42

5

 20 minutes

 No limit

 5 clothespins for each participant

Silly hair

Objectives

Allow group members to communicate with different people and create a relaxing and pleasant atmosphere.

How to play

1. Each member should be given five clothespins (the number may vary depending on the desired length of the game).

2. Each member should then invite one person from the crowd to be their opponent.

3. They will play "rock, paper, scissors", and the winner should gently clip a clothespin to the other's hair.

4. Members should then invite another group member to be their opponent. They should try to play with someone new each time.

5. Once a group member is able to clip all five of their clothespins to other members, then they win.

6. The game can continue until multiple members have clipped all of their clothespins, or even until all of the clothespins have been attached to a single person.

Reminders and precautions

Remind group members to be careful where they attach the clothespins to the others to avoid pinching or pain.

Debriefing

1. The facilitator should gather the first member who attached all their clothespins to others (the first one to win) and the member who has the most clothespins in their hair to share their feelings.

2. After the game, the facilitator can gather the group members to take photos together to remember their "silly hair".

Rock, paper, scissors

You lose!

6

 20 minutes

 Preferably 10

 Clothespins, blindfold, foam or paper sticks, timer

Reminders and precautions

1. The facilitator must be sure to pay attention to the stick material. A styrofoam stick is recommended to avoid injury to other members when the blindfolded member swings the stick.
2. Obstacles must be removed from the venue to avoid injury.
3. A larger room is recommended to increase the degree or intensity of movements and fun of the game.

Debriefing

1. Help members learn how to protect themselves by actively participating in the game.
2. This game encourages the creativity of the group members. If the rules of the game are not clearly specified, then the group members may use different ways to pin the clothespins onto the blindfolded member's clothes. For instance, some members may work together to distract the blindfolded member and let other members place the clothespin on them. This game helps members learn the spirit of cooperation.

Clothespin war

Objectives

Allow group members to move around and interact with one another to warm up and create a relaxing atmosphere.

How to play

1. All group members should stand in a circle.

2. The facilitator should select one member to stand in the middle of the circle and cover their eyes while holding a foam (or paper) stick. The other group members should be given one (or more) clothespins.

3. When the game starts, other team members should quickly (but gently) clip the clothespins onto the blindfolded member's clothes. To stop them, the blindfolded group member should slowly swing the foam (or paper) stick around themselves.

4. Once a group member is hit by the foam (or paper) stick, they will be out from the game and should move to the side.

5. After a set amount of time has passed or all members have been tagged out with the stick, the facilitator should count the number of clothespins on the blindfolded member.

6. Group members should take turns being the one in the middle.

7

 15 minutes

 No limit

 None

Give me ten or five

Objectives

Enhance interactions between members and create an atmosphere of mutual support.

How to play

Method 1: High ten (or double high five)

1. The game facilitator should lead the members to shout slogans used for greeting that inspire and enhance group cohesion, such as "Good Morning", "How are you?", "Come on", and "Good luck!" The slogans should be said while giving double high fives (i.e., high ten, using both hands).

2. Each group member should then move around, giving double high fives with other group members while simultaneously shouting a slogan.

3. The game ends when each group member has given a double high five to every other member.

Method 2: High five

1. Group members should form a straight line and place their hands on the shoulders of the member in front of them to form a chain.

2. The game facilitator is the starting point or head of the chain.

3. When the game starts, the game facilitator first turns around and uses one hand to give a high five to the second member. Then, the facilitator continues to move down the line and give a high five to each member down the chain.

4. The second member should follow the facilitator and give a high five to the member behind them and then continue down the chain. Then the third member should follow them and so on.

5. By doing this, members will move to make an inward circle and every member needs to move forward until they can give a high five to all other members.

Reminders and precautions

None.

Debriefing

1. Help members understand that everyone needs support and encouragement.

2. Discuss how members can use certain actions to show support and encouragement and strengthen the spirit of the group.

When the game starts, the facilitator first turns around and gives a high five to the group member behind them, followed by the next group member, and continuing down the line. Each group member should do the same, giving high fives to each of the other members down the line.

8

Evolution

20 minutes

16–20
(it is better to play this game with an even number of participants; if there is an odd number, then one group member should be selected to be a judge)

None

Objectives

Allow members to move around, interact with others, and create a fun and relaxing atmosphere.

How to play

1. This game is about the four stages of "evolution": egg, chicken, phoenix, and then human.

2. The four stages should be demonstrated with different movements: the egg is shown by squatting down; the chicken is shown by kneeling with hands on the waist and elbows "flapping"; the phoenix is shown by bending down with hands placed on top of the head; the human is shown by standing up straight with arms raised into the air.

3. All members should start as eggs. They should then play "rock, paper, scissors" with the group members around them (also eggs).

4. The winning egg will become a chicken, while the losing egg will remain an egg. The winning chicken can then move around to find another chicken to play "rock, paper, scissors", and the winner will become a phoenix, while the loser will remain a chicken. The phoenix should then find another phoenix to play with. The winner will become a human being, while the loser will remain a phoenix. After winning their way to becoming a human, that human can leave the game and stand on the side-lines to clap for other group members still playing to encourage them.

5. Notably, only those in the same evolution stage can play "rock, paper, scissors" together. They can see who is at the same stage based on their movements and position as well as by saying their stage out loud.

Reminders and precautions

This game is not suitable for older people or those with limited mobility.

Debriefing

None.

Egg   Chicken   Phoenix   Human

All members start as eggs. They will then play "rock, paper, scissors" with the other group members around them. The winner will evolve to the next stage.

9

15 minutes

No limit
(it is better to play this game with an even number of participants; if there is an odd number, then one group member should be selected to be a judge)

None

Spider and snake

Objectives

Improve contact and interaction between group members as well as test their reactions and inspire them.

How to play

1. Group members should be divided into two teams. The members of each team will form a line, facing the members of the opposite team.

2. The game facilitator should assign one team as the "spider" and the other team as the "snake".

3. Each member of a team should then extend their right thumbs to touch the right thumbs of a member of the opposing team.

4. When the game facilitator calls "spider", the members of the spider team should immediately try to catch the hand of the opponent, while the members of the snake team should immediately move their hands away to avoid being caught.

5. After counting how many were caught, the game resets. The game facilitator can then call "snake", and the process is reversed. This can continue for several rounds. Group members can keep playing across from the same opponent or they can switch opponents.

6. The game can be changed by asking the members to place their right hand above their opponent's shoulder or head. In this variation, the members must touch the shoulder or head of their opponent when their team name is called, while the opposite team members must move their shoulders or heads away. After playing one round, the game facilitator may change the names of the teams to other animals (e.g., cockroaches vs crocodiles, pandas vs penguins, or butterflies vs buffalo).

Reminders and precautions

If the game is changed to involve touching the shoulder and head, then the members may run to get away from the other team. Thus, playing in a spacious indoor venue or open and flat grassland is recommended.

Debriefing

None.

Each member of a team should extend their right thumbs to touch the right thumbs of a member of the opposing team.

When the game facilitator calls the name of a team, the members of that team should immediately try to catch the hand of their opponent.

10

 15–20 minutes

 No limit
(it is better to play this game with an even number of participants; if there is an odd number, then one group member should be selected to be a judge)

 None

Body "rock, paper, scissors"

Objectives

Increase members' activity level and create a relaxing atmosphere.

How to play

1. Each member needs to find a partner to play the game.

2. Before starting the game, the game facilitator should demonstrate how to use the body posture to represent "rock", "paper", and "scissors".

3. When the game starts, the two members should be facing away from each other.

4. The game facilitator should count "1, 2, 3", and the two members will jump and turn around to show their selected body posture of either "rock", "paper", or "scissors". The game stops when one member wins two rounds.

5. The game may be changed by asking the members to create their own creative or funny body postures to represent "rock", "paper", and "scissors".

6. This game may also be changed through competition between two teams. The team with most winning member wins.

Reminders and precautions

Each partner group should maintain adequate distance from the other groups to ensure they have enough space to jump into the different postures. This game is recommended to be played in a spacious venue.

Debriefing

None.

Rock

Paper

Scissors

Get ready...

Jump and turn...

Win!

11

 15–20 minutes

 No limit
(it is better to play this game with an even number of participants; if there is an odd number, then one group member should be selected to be a judge)

 None

Special "rock, paper, scissors"

Objectives

Create a relaxing atmosphere, enhance interaction between group members, and allow each member to express their creativity.

How to play

1. The game facilitator should ask all group members to create their own body posture to represent "rock", "paper", and "scissors" using only their feet.

2. Each member should then find a partner and use their created posture to play "rock, paper, scissors". The game stops when one member wins two rounds.

3. The member who loses should use one or both hands to touch the shoulders of the winning members.

4. The winning member (with their previous opponents touching their back) should then play against another group member. This should continue until all of the group members are touching someone's back except the winner.

5. The game may be changed by asking members to create their own "facial expressions" or "other special body movements" to represent the "rock", "paper", and "scissors".

Reminders and precautions

Each partner group should maintain an adequate distance from other groups. This game is recommended to be played in a spacious venue.

Debriefing

None.

56

12

 10 minutes

 No limit
(it is better to play this game with an even number of participants; if there is an odd number, then one group member should be selected to be a judge)

 None

Pushing the palms

Objectives

Encourage and enhance interactions between group members and create a relaxing atmosphere.

How to play

1. Each group member should find a partner. They should stand facing each other with their arms outstretched and palms touching those of the other person.

2. After the facilitator counts down or says start, the two members should try to push each other away. If a member moves one foot or both feet, then they lose.

3. The winning group member should then find another member to play with, while the group members who have lost should stand on the side-lines and cheer for the others.

Reminders and precautions

1. This game is not suitable for members who feel uncomfortable coming into contact with others in the group.
2. Group members should be reminded about personal safety while they are pushing others.

Debriefing

None.

13

 20 minutes

 8–10

 None

Bing, bang, wah

Objectives

Allow interaction between group members and enhance their ability to concentrate and show a rapid response.

How to play

1. All group members should sit in a circle.
2. The facilitator should choose one group member to start ("A"). Member A should point their index finger at another group member ("B") and say "bing".
3. Then Member B should immediately point at another member ("C") and say either "bing" or "bang".
4. If Member C receives a "bing", then they will need to repeat Step 3, saying either "bing" or "bang". However, if Member C receives a "bang", then members sitting on either side of Member C should respond immediately by raising both hands and saying "wah".
5. Member C will then continue the game starting with pointing at another group member and saying "bing". They should keep playing until a member responds incorrectly.
6. If someone says "bang" and points in the air, then all group members should respond by raising both hands and saying "wah".

Reminders and precautions

This game can be played online by replacing the finger pointing with saying another group member's name.

Debriefing

1. Try to help members stay focused and encourage them to pay attention to the changes in the surrounding environment.
2. Discuss with the group how each of them felt about needing to stay aware of what other group members were doing so they could respond correctly.

14

 20 minutes

 10–15

 None

Good turtle, bad turtle

Objectives

Create a relaxing atmosphere, allow group members to express their true temperament, test their reactions, and encourage them to get to know each other.

How to play

1. All group members should stand in a circle.

2. The facilitator should choose one group member to start ("A"). Member A should point to another group member ("B") and say either "good turtle" or "bad turtle" and ask them to do a simple action (e.g., "good turtle, raise both hands" or "good turtle, touch your head").

3. When Member A says "good turtle", Member B should execute the command as requested. However, if Member A says "bad turtle", Member B should do the opposite action (e.g., turning to the left instead of right, standing up instead of sitting down). If the command does not have an opposite action (e.g., spinning), then Member B does not need to do anything.

4. Members who do the incorrect actions lose. If the member executes the action correctly, then they should point to another member to give a new order until someone makes a wrong move. Once a member loses, another round can be started again by the loser. If the member loses a certain number of times (the number of times can be customised), they must pull both of their ears and repeatedly say for half a minute (or a set number of times) "I will be a better turtle."

Reminders and precautions

Any animal with two syllables can be used (e.g., bunny, panda, lizard, otter, puppy, etc.); however, it would be best to avoid animals that the participants could be afraid of and those with distinct links to gender or race so all participants feel included in the game.

Debriefing

None.

15

 15 minutes

 No limit
(it is better to play
this game with many
participants)

 None

Reminders and precautions

1. This game is best played with participants who will understand monetary amounts and sums.

2. The assigned amount of money assigned for different items may be changed at any time.

3. To increase difficulty, group members can be told not to talk so they have to determine the amount of each person based on what they are wearing.

4. The facilitator should pay special attention to whether certain members tend to be unable to join a group or are excluded.

5. Another level of difficulty can be added by having an item (e.g., laundry detergent) that the group members need to guess the estimated price of and then form a group to come up with that amount.

Debriefing

Help members understand how this game reflects how every member has personal characteristics or strengths that can contribute to the group.

One dollar, five cents

Objectives

Facilitate interactions between group members, promote a relaxing atmosphere, and improve communication within the group.

How to play

1. The game facilitator should assign dollar amounts to each group member based on various articles of clothing they are wearing (e.g., a person's total amount will be based on what they are wearing) The facilitator should explain what items are worth, for example, glasses (worth $1), jeans (50¢), sweater (25¢), socks ($2), belt (75¢), shirt or dress with buttons ($1), shirt or dress with pockets ($2), etc. Thus, based on these example amounts, someone wearing jeans, a sweater, and socks will be worth $2.75.

2. Once each person is assigned a dollar amount, the game facilitator should say an amount of money (e.g., $10) and group members will need to group themselves to come up with that amount. Members who are able to form a group corresponding to that amount should immediately sit or kneel. The fastest group wins.

16

 20 minutes

 No limit
(it is better to play
this game with many
participants)

 Rope or paper strips

Step on the tail

Objectives

Allow group members to move around and interact with one another, as well as create an active atmosphere.

How to play

1. Each member is given a rope (or a paper strip) that reaches from the ground (at least 2 cm dragging on the ground) up to a position on their back where it can be fastened. (The rope or paper strip can be measured and cut at the time of the game if necessary.)

2. Group members should then tuck one end of the rope or paper strip into the back of their pants, waistband, or a back pocket (or it can be taped to their back). (Do not pin to clothing.)

3. When the game starts, members should move around to try and step on the "tails" of other members so they pull off, while also keeping their own intact.

4. Once a group member loses their tail, they should move to the side-lines and cheer for the remaining members.

5. The members who have not lost their tails after a set amount of time win.

Reminders and precautions

1. This may not be a good game to play with participants with long skirts or clothing that could be stepped on or pulled off.

2. The facilitator must carefully control the atmosphere of the game given that the members might bump into each other. The game should be stopped if necessary.

3. The size of the activity area can be adjusted to increase the difficulty level.

Debriefing

None.

17

 15 minutes

 10–15

 Chairs
(the number of chairs should be equal to the number of participants)

Come back!

Objectives

Help members warm-up and strengthen their sense of involvement.

How to play

1. The chairs should be arranged in a circle facing inward. Each group member should sit in a chair.

2. The game facilitator should choose one group member ("A") to stand inside the circle, leaving one seat vacant.

3. When the game starts, other members need to prevent Member A from sitting down by moving around the circle in a clockwise direction to occupy the chair before they can sit.

4. If a seated team member wants to change the direction (from clockwise to counter-clockwise), they will not transfer to the next chair but just place their hand on the vacant chair (indicating to the person on the other side of the empty chair to move back into it).

5. When Member A is able to sit, the member who fails to fill the empty chair is the next person in the middle.

Reminders and precautions

1. When members move around the circle to sit on the next chair, they may bump into others, which may cause injuries.

2. In case of a dangerous situation or aggressive actions, the game facilitator will need to stop the game.

3. Group members may come into physical contact with others while competing for the chairs. Thus, this game is not suitable for those who may feel uncomfortable being in close contact with others.

Debriefing

Help members understand that if group members operate collectively and cooperatively, then they can easily prevent Member A from sitting on the chair.

18

 20 minutes

 Preferably 10–15

 Chairs

Reminders and precautions

1. When providing an order, the number of group members with the announced characteristics needs to be more than two.

2. The facilitator should pay attention to members who might bump into others while moving and running to find another seat.

3. The group members who must leave their seat cannot go back to the same seat or sit on the two adjacent seats.

Debriefing

1. Help members understand that if they interact more, then they can better break down psychological barriers.

2. Changing seats can help enhance communication in the group and encourage members to sit next to people they do not know.

3. Members may utilise this chance to remember the personal characteristics of other group members (e.g., eye colour, hair colour, braces, etc.).

A big wind blows

Objectives

Facilitate interaction within the group, help group members get to know more people, and teach them to pay attention to the personal characteristics of others.

How to play

1. The chairs should be arranged in a circle facing inward, and the number of chairs should be one less than the number of group members.

2. All members must find and sit on a chair, leaving one member without a seat. This group member should stand in the middle of the circle and say "A big wind blows", to which the other members should respond "What will blow away?"

3. The group member without a seat will then give an order by saying one feature, such as "The wind blows away those with long hair" or "The wind blows away those wearing blue shirts". With this order, all group members having this characteristic should stand up and move to find another chair to sit in. Others without this characteristic should stay seated.

4. The member giving the order will take this opportunity to find a chair to sit down while the other team members change positions.

5. The member who does not find a new seat will repeat Steps 2–4 for the next round and issue another order (e.g., "The wind blows away those with glasses").

19

A small wind blows

 20 minutes

 Preferably 10–15

 Chairs

Reminders and precautions

1. When providing an order, the number of members with the announced characteristics (or in this case the lack of the characteristic) should be more than two.

2. The facilitator should pay attention to members who might bump into others while moving and running to find another seat.

3. The group members who must leave their seat cannot go back to the same seat or sit on the two adjacent seats.

Debriefing

1. Help members understand that if they interact more, then they can better break down psychological barriers.

2. Changing seats can help enhance communication in the group and encourage members to sit next to people they do not know.

3. Members may utilise this chance to remember the personal characteristics of other group members (e.g., eye colour, hair colour, braces, etc.).

Objectives

Encourage interaction between group members, change seats to get to know more new friends, and learn to pay attention to the personal characteristics of others.

How to play

1. This game is played similar to "A big wind blows" (Game 18). The only difference is that the member without a seat can choose to say either "A big wind blows" or "A small wind blows".

2. If the order is "A small wind blows", then the seated group members have to react oppositely. For example, if after saying "A small wind blows", they say "The wind blows away those with a watch", then members with this characteristic should stay seated on the chair, but those without will have to move and run to find another chair.

20

 15 minutes

 15–20

 Chairs

The boat captain

Objectives

Allow members to walk around and change positions as well as create a relaxing atmosphere.

How to play

1. The chairs should be arranged in a circle facing inward, and the number of chairs should be one less than the number of members.

2. The game facilitator should pick a category and each group member should pick a type of this category to represent themselves. For example, if the category is animals, then members can choose to be elephants, lions, etc., or if the category is flowers, then members can choose to be daffodils, lilacs, etc.

3. One member will be designated the boat captain and should stand in the middle, while the other members stay seated.

4. When the game starts, the designated member should say "I am the boat captain! We need to avoid the flood!"

5. Then, they should call up the different animals, flowers, etc. the other members have chosen. These members should then stand up and line up behind the captain with their hands on the shoulders of the member in front of them. The line will coil around the inner circle.

6. After a number of people are lined up, the captain should say "The flood is coming!" Then, the captain and all the members lined up behind them have to find a chair and sit down.

7. The member who fails to find a seat will become the boat captain in the next round.

Reminders and precautions

The facilitator will need to pay attention to members as they might bump into others while running to find a seat.

Debriefing

None.

21

 15 minutes

 10–15

 Chairs, equipment to play music

Invite friends

Objectives

Allow members to walk around and change positions as well as to create a relaxing atmosphere.

How to play

1. The chairs should be arranged in a circle facing inward, and the number of chairs should be one more than the number of group members so there is one empty chair when all group members are sitting.

2. The game facilitator should then start to play music.

3. While the music is playing, the two members sitting on either side of the vacant seat should stand up and invite any member who is sitting to come and sit in the empty seat. When they come to the seat, all three should sit down at the same time.

4. The two members sitting on either side of the newly vacated seat should then stand up and invite another member to change seats, repeating Step 3.

5. Step 3 should be repeated until the game facilitator stops the music, the members who are still standing when the music stops lose.

Reminders and precautions

Group members should be reminded to be careful not to bump into others while moving or running to their new seats.

Debriefing

Help members share their feelings about being invited or not invited to switch seats and encourage them to take other initiatives to connect with other group members.

22

 15–20 minutes

 15–20

 None

Who is the leader?

Objectives

Allow group members to work together and encourage interactions to create a relaxing atmosphere.

How to play

1. All group members should stand in a circle and select one member to be responsible for "guessing" who the leader is. This member needs to leave the venue for a moment.

2. Other group members should then decide who should be the leader. The leader will lead all group members to do some action and will be the one to initiate any change in the action (e.g., clapping hands, touching the head, raising hands, stepping in place, etc.).

3. All members will have to follow the leader in doing the same action they are doing.

4. Before the guessing member comes back into the venue, the leader should start an action and all members should begin to follow them and doing the same action.

5. The guessing member should then come back, stand in the middle of the circle, and observe the members' actions to discover who the leader is. The guessing member can turn around in the circle to see everyone.

6. The leader should freely change the actions, trying to avoid the guessing member seeing who is initiating the change. Other members must follow the new actions collectively and immediately.

7. The guessing member wins if they can discover who the leader is.

8. If there are quite a few participants, then the game facilitator can choose two members to guess.

Reminders and precautions

None.

Debriefing

Discuss with group members the importance of paying attention to body language.

23

 15–20 minutes

 No limit
(it is better to play
this game with an
even number of
participants; if there is
an odd number, then
one group member
should be selected to
be a judge)

 None

Reminders and precautions

Group members may need to be
reminded to be careful when turning
around.

Debriefing

None.

Changing the weather

Objectives

Enhance group cohesion and test the reaction times and agility of each
group member.

How to play

1. Group members should be divided into two teams (Team A and
   Team B). Members of each team should then form a line facing the
   members of the opposite team.

2. Members of Team A represent hot weather, while those of Team B
   represent cold weather.

3. When the game facilitator says "Winter is coming", the group
   members in Team A should quickly turn around so their backs
   are towards the other team. Group members in Team B should
   not move.

4. When the game facilitator says "Summer is coming", the group
   members in Team B should quickly turn around so their backs
   are towards the other team. Group members in Team A should
   not move.

5. When the game facilitator says "Autumn is coming", none of the
   members of either team should move.

6. When the game facilitator says "A typhoon is coming", the group
   members of both teams should turn around so their backs are
   towards the other team.

7. The game facilitator can speed up the pace or freely change the
   order of the instructions. The slowest members or those incorrectly
   doing the action can be identified and "frozen" or they can be
   taken out of the game to cheer for the others from the side-lines.

24

 15–20 minutes

 No limit

 None

Disaster in the forest

Objectives

Allow group members to move around, make connections with other members, and strengthen group interaction.

How to play

1. The group members should be divided into teams of three, except for one group member who the facilitator should assign to give the first command to everyone else (Member "A").

2. In the teams of three, two members should stand up, raise their hands, and hold the hands together to form a "tree". They are the "tree members". The third member of the group is the "squirrel member" who has to kneel under the tree as a "squirrel".

3. If Member A says "Earthquake in the forest", the squirrel member of each team should not move, but the two tree members have to separate and find another tree member to join with, and then they need to stand over a different squirrel. After calling the command, Member A should also take the opportunity to become a tree member, joining up with another tree. The member who does not pair with another tree member will become the new Member A to give a command in the next round.

4. If Member A says "Flooding in the forest", the tree members should not move, but the squirrel member has to move away immediately to hide under another tree. After calling the command, Member A should also take the opportunity to replace someone as a squirrel member. The squirrel member who cannot find a new tree will become the new Member A to give a command in the next round.

5. If Member A says "Fire in the forest", everyone must move. They can either find another member to make a tree or become a squirrel. After calling the command, Member A should replace someone's position as a tree or squirrel as soon as possible. The member who cannot find a group to be a tree or squirrel, then they will become the new Member A to give a command in the next round.

Reminders and precautions

This game is better played in a large and open space.

Debriefing

None.

25

 20 minutes

 24–32

 Newspaper or rope

Earthquakes

Objectives

Allow group members to move around, promote their interactions with each other, and improve their flexibility.

How to play

1. The group members should be divided into four teams, with six to eight members in a team.

2. Members of each team should stand inside an area marked by a newspaper or a rope. This designates their "country".

3. Each team should choose a country name. Group members should be reminded that the space in each area can only accommodate six to eight members.

4. To start the game, the game facilitator should say that a country is having an earthquake. Then, the members in that country should immediately flee and try to stand inside the areas of other countries.

5. The members who cannot safely stand inside the area of another country will be out of the game. The game facilitator should then continue calling other country names.

6. The team with the most number of members remaining at the end of the game wins.

Reminders and precautions

This game should be played in a flat and open space (e.g., an outdoor grassland or an auditorium). Members should be careful to avoid accidentally pushing or running into other members.

Debriefing

Help members share their feelings about needing to switch countries and what it was like to not be accommodated in other countries after the earthquake.

26

15 minutes

No limit
(it is better to play this game with an even number of participants; if there is an odd number, then one group member should be selected to be a judge)

None

Mirror dance

Objectives

Increase and enhance interactions between group members and test their reaction times.

How to play

1. Each group member should get a partner, and they should stand facing each other.

2. One member should be designated the leader. Any movement or action they do, their partner should mirror.

3. The leader can gradually increase the level of difficulty of the movement their partner has to mimic.

4. This should be repeated with the other member being the leader.

Reminders and precautions

This game can be played online.

Debriefing

Help members understand that freeing themselves is essential in modelling the actions of others. Discuss how this could also apply to learning a skill from others.

27

 20 minutes

 10–15

 None

Protect the general

Objectives

Allow group members to warm up and move around, create a relaxing atmosphere, and strengthen teamwork.

How to play

1. The group facilitator should select one member to be the general, seven to eight participants to be the soldiers, and two to be the traitors.

2. When the game starts, everyone should move around. The soldiers should be instructed to protect the general and prevent the traitors from catching them.

3. When the traitors touch the soldiers, the soldiers have to kneel and cannot move. The soldiers can only move again after being touched by the general.

4. The game will end if the traitor catches the general.

Reminders and precautions

This game should be played in a flat and open space (e.g., an outdoor grassland or a large auditorium). Members should be careful to avoid accidentally pushing other members.

Debriefing

Help members understand the importance of cooperation and focusing on a collective goal.

28

 20 minutes

 20

 None

Sticky beans

Objectives

Allow group members to interact and get to know each other.

How to play

1. Each group member should get a partner. They should stand next to each other at a distance from other teams.

2. The facilitator should select one pair to start. One of them (Member A) should run around and the other (Member B) should chase them.

3. To escape, Member A should run and stick to a different team and call out the name of one of the team members. That team member now becomes the new Member A and the target being chased by Member B.

4. If Member A is caught by Member B, then they have to switch places, so Member A is now chasing Member B. The member being chased can then escape by sticking to another team and making one of them the new target.

Reminders and precautions

This game should be played in a flat and open space (e.g., an outdoor grassland or a large auditorium). Members should be careful when running around to avoid bumping into others.

Debriefing

None.

29

 15 minutes

 No limit

 None

Tapping hands

Objectives

Create a relaxing atmosphere and test members' reaction times.

How to play

1. All group members should sit in a circle.

2. Each member should raise their left hand out to the side with the palm facing up. Then, they should raise their right hand out to the side with the palm facing down above the left palm of the person next to them.

3. When the game facilitator says "1, 2, 3, Go!", the group members should use their right hand to try to tap the other person's left hand, while simultaneously avoiding their own left hand being tapped.

4. The game can also be changed by asking one member to pick a "Go" word. The facilitator should then tell a story and at some point use that word. When group members hear this word, they should try to tap the other group member's hand as soon as possible, while also protecting their own left hand.

5. An alternative to this is also explained in Chapter 2 of Part I.

Reminders and precautions

Members should be reminded to be gentle when trying to tap the hands of other group members.

Debriefing

None.

30

 10 minutes

 No limit

 None

Look and clap your hands

Objectives

Test members' reaction times and create a cooperative atmosphere.

How to play

1. The facilitator should stand with their arms stretched straight out in front of them with their hands facing each other. They will move both hands to face different directions so that the palms can be facing upward, downward, or towards each other.

2. The group members should look at and pay attention to the hand movements of the facilitator. When their palms are facing each other, the group members should clap their hands once.

3. The facilitator should then repeat the movements, speeding up gradually and making fake moves from time to time to trick members to clap their hands.

4. The game may end when the atmosphere reaches a climax.

5. There are additional considerations for this game in Chapter 2 of Part I.

Reminders and precautions

This game can be played online.

Debriefing

None.

31

 20 minutes

 12–15

 Playing cards

Playing cards on the head

Objectives

Promote and enhance interactions between group members and create a relaxing atmosphere.

How to play

1. Group members should sit in a circle. The group facilitator should let each member pick a playing card. They should not look at their card, but should instead hold it up to their forehead facing out to the rest of the group.

2. Each member should then specify a difficult, interesting, or funny action to be executed by others (for example, doing 10 push-ups, drinking water without hands, etc.).

3. After all members have provided a proposed action, everyone should look at their own card and set it down.

4. The member with the smallest card number has to do the action proposed by the member with the largest card number.

Reminders and precautions
None.

Debriefing
None.

32

 20–25 minutes

 10–15

 Chairs
(enough for each
group member)

Protect the chair

Objectives

Allow group members to move around, create a relaxing atmosphere, and strengthen teamwork.

How to play

Method 1:

1. The chairs should be arranged randomly around the venue.

2. All group members should sit in a chair. The facilitator should designate one member ("A") to stand at one side of the venue, leaving one seat vacant.

3. When the game starts, all members should leave their chairs and move around to try and fill any empty chairs, while preventing Member A from sitting on a chair.

4. If Member A is able to find a chair to sit down, they win.

5. The game facilitator will then choose another Member A to compete for a chair.

Method 2:

1. Similar to Method 1.

2. The only difference is that the group members can pick up and move the chairs to increase the difficulty for Member A to find a chair to sit in.

Reminders and precautions

This game should be played in a spacious and unobstructed area. Members should be reminded to be careful to avoid accidentally bumping into others.

Debriefing

1. Help members understand that they can work together to stop something "negative".

2. Discuss with the group what it felt like to be Member A during this game when everyone else was working together.

33

 20–25 minutes

 15–20

 A large, colourful piece of cloth or bed-sheet, balloons or small rubber balls

Rainbow umbrella

Objectives

Create a relaxing atmosphere and strengthen teamwork.

How to play

Method 1:

1. The group members should be instructed to hold the edges of the large and colourful cloth (perceived as an open rainbow umbrella).

2. A balloon (or rubber ball) should be placed on the umbrella. Then, the members will raise and lower their part of the umbrella to send the balloon or ball to the opposing side while avoiding the balloon or ball from going outside of the umbrella.

3. The number of balloons can be increased to increase the level of difficulty.

Method 2:

1. Four to six members should be instructed to hold and raise the rainbow umbrella.

2. Other members should try to move under the umbrella from one side to the other. The members holding the umbrella should try to stop them from passing under and cover them up with the umbrella.

Method 3:

1. Four to six members should be instructed to hold and raise the rainbow umbrella.

2. Other members should stand under the umbrella. When the umbrella is raised, they should try to escape, and the members holding the umbrella should try to prevent them from escaping.

Reminders and precautions

This game should be played in a spacious and unobstructed area. It is suitable for people with intellectual disabilities, children, and families.

Debriefing

None.

34

 20–25 minutes

 10–15

 None

Put your right hand in

Objectives

Allow group members to stretch their muscles and create a relaxing and positive atmosphere.

How to play

1. Group members should stand in a circle.

2. The game facilitator should teach the group members to sing the following song and lead them to do the movements while singing along.

> Put your right hand in *(move your right hand towards the middle of the circle)*,
> put your right hand out *(move your right hand outside of the circle)*
> and shake it all around *(shake your hand)*
> OH BooGee BooGee BooGee *(Freely moving the body)*
>
> Put your left hand in, put your left hand out, and shake it all around
> *(movements with the left hand)*
> OH BooGee BooGee BooGee *(Freely moving the body)*
>
> Put your right shoulder in, put your right shoulder out, and shake it all around
> *(movements with the right shoulder)*
> OH BooGee BooGee BooGe *(Freely moving the body)*
>
> Put your left shoulder in, put your left shoulder out, and shake it all around
> *(movements with the left shoulder)*
> OH BooGee BooGee BooGee *(Freely moving the body)*
>
> Put your right hip in, put your right hip out, and shake it all around
> *(movements with the right hip)*
> OH BooGee BooGee BooGee *(Freely moving the body)*
>
> Put your left hip in, put your left hip out, and shake it all around
> *(movements with the left hip)*
> OH BooGee BooGee BooGee *(Freely moving the body)*
>
> Put your right leg in, put your right leg out, and shake it all around
> *(movements with the right leg)*
> OH BooGee BooGee BooGee *(Freely moving the body)*
>
> Put your left leg in, put your left leg out, and shake it all around
> *(movements with the left leg)*
> OH BooGee BooGee BooGee *(Freely moving the body)*

Reminders and precautions

While executing the movements, the game facilitator should try to keep the atmosphere fun and lively.

Debriefing

None.

Put your head head in, put your head head out, and shake it all around *(movements with the head)*
OH BooGee BooGee BooGee *(Freely moving the body)*

Put your whole body in, put your whole body out and shake it all around *(movements with the whole body)*
OH BooGee BooGee BooGee *(Freely moving the body)*

Put your neighbour in *(drag your neighbour inside the circle)*,
put your neighbour out *(pull your neighbour out of the circle)*,
and shake them all around *(gently shake them)*
OH BooGee BooGee BooGee *(Freely moving the body)*

Put your right hand in

Put your right shoulder in

Put your right leg in

OH BooGee BooGee BooGee

2

Mutual Understanding Games

35

 20 minutes

 Preferably 20

 3–5 small or plastic toys or furry dolls

Reminders and precautions

1. When throwing the toys, members should be reminded that they need to make eye contact with the other member catching the toy.

2. Group members should use a good throwing technique, tossing the toy slowly and from a low angle.

3. Throwing a ball is discouraged in this game, as it can be easily thrown far away and may also easily hurt the group members catching it.

Debriefing

Help members understand that:
1. People like to set limits on their own actions.

2. People can break through their own limits through group cooperation and setting a common goal.

Throwing toys

Objectives

Allow members to introduce themselves and get to know each other, create a relaxing atmosphere, and enhance group cohesion.

How to play

Method 1:

1. Members should form a circle and share their names and nicknames.

2. The game facilitator should throw a toy to a group member. That member needs to throw the toy to another member until all members have received the toy once. The last member who catches the toy needs to throw it back to the game facilitator to finish one round.

3. While throwing the toy, the members should (a) make eye contact, (b) call the name of the member to whom they are going to throw the toy, (c) throw the toy to the group member whose name they called, (d) the last catcher throws the toy back to the facilitator.

4. Members cannot throw the toy to the member sitting next to them.

5. To start, each group member will throw the toy to the same person in each round. The game facilitator should count total time to finish one round. Then, the members will be asked to think and discuss how to speed up the finishing time for the second round.

6. After a few rounds, the game facilitator can throw some more toys, so that more members can throw the toys simultaneously.

7. Additional details and considerations for this game are explained in Chapter 2 of Part I. There the game is titled "Chicken thrower".

Method 2:

1. For this method, the game facilitator should prepare the same number of toys as the number of participants.

2. When each member receives a toy, they should toss the toy up and catch it themselves. Other more complex tosses can then be requested. For example, members can throw the toy up and have to clap their hands, touch their chest three times, stand with one leg, or close one eye before they catch the toy again.

Method 3:

1. Another way is to ask each member to find a partner. Then they should throw their toys to each other. Alternatively, the members can form groups of four and stand at the corner of a square to throw the toy to the member at the diagonal corner. Members can also be asked to form groups of eight.

2. If the game facilitator notices that members only find familiar members as their partners, they can encourage them to be partners with other unfamiliar group members.

Method 4:

1. The game can also be changed by asking all members to stand in a circle and selecting four members to stand inside the circle.

2. Then, all members will throw their toys to these four members. The member who catches the most toys wins.

36

 20 minutes

 No limit

 None

Find the order

Objectives

Help members get to know other members' personal information and build up team spirit.

How to play

1. The game facilitator should select a characteristic and ask all group members to arrange in an appropriate order based on that characteristic. For example, the members must arrange in order based on their student ID number (smallest to the largest), their birthday date (the date and month of the birth date, not the year), their English surnames (alphabetically), and so on.

2. All members should start by standing scattered around the venue and are not allowed to speak. They can only communicate with one another through body language.

3. The whole group needs to think of the fastest way to arrange themselves in the correct order. The game facilitator can also ask the whole group to set a time limit to complete the game. Once all of the group members are lined up in the order they think is correct, the game facilitator should check whether the order is correct.

4. The game can be changed by using a group competition format. The fastest group to arrange in the correct order wins.

Reminders and precautions

None.

Debriefing

Help members share their feeling about needing to use body language to communicate with one another. Encourage members to take note of other members' information, such as birthdays for recall later.

37

 15 minutes

 Preferably 8–10

 None

I am a teddy bear

Objectives

Remember members' names based on their voice alone.

How to play

1. Group members should start by standing in a circle.

2. The game facilitator should pick one group member ("A") to stand in the middle of the circle. Member A should close their eyes, while the other members slowly walk around to change positions in the circle.

3. Member A will then shout "stop", and all members will need to stop moving. Keeping their eyes closed, Member A should then point to another member ("B"). Member B will then shout "I am a teddy bear".

4. Member A needs to guess who Member B is. If correct, then Member B will become the person to guess in the next round. If not, then Member B should shout "I am a teddy bear" again, and Member A can try to guess again. They have three chances to guess correctly.

5. If Member A does not guess correctly after three tries, then the game facilitator will choose a new member to guess.

6. Alternatively, if Member A does not guess the identity of Member B correctly, then they can be instructed to point to a different member ("C"), who will also shout "I am a teddy bear". Member A will have three tries to guess who they are. The game facilitator can decide how many tries they get to guess one person as well as how many times they can point to someone new.

7. Group members can also try to use a fake voice to add difficulty.

Reminders and precautions

Before the game starts, the game facilitator needs to ask all members to say their names first.

Debriefing

None.

38

 15 minutes

 10–15

 None

Two actions, one mind

Objectives

Enhance mutual understanding within the group and improve their active listening skills.

How to play

1. All members should sit down and form a circle.

2. The game facilitator should suggest topics or characteristics for the members to share about themselves, such as their name, school name, work nature, hobbies, favourite food, etc.

3. The group members should then introduce themselves to the person to their left, while simultaneously listening to the person to their right introducing themselves.

4. Upon completion, each member takes a turn to share with the whole group the personal information of the member sitting to their right.

Reminders and precautions

None.

Debriefing

Discuss the concept of multi-tasking along with the pros and cons of speaking while trying to pay attention to others.

39

 15 minutes

 10–15

 Newspaper

Bop the fools

Objectives

Help group members learn each other's names, increase interactions, and test their reaction times.

How to play

1. The game facilitator should make a stick or tube by rolling up a piece of newspaper.

2. One group member ("A") should be asked to hold the newspaper stick and use it to gently hit ("bop") the heads of other members.

3. The other members should stand side-by-side in groups of two and form a large circle.

4. When the game starts, Member A should go up to a group member ("B") and try to gently bop their head. Before Member B is bopped, their partner should immediately call the name of another group member ("C").

5. After Member C's name is called, Member A should change their target from Member B to Member C. To prevent Member C from getting bopped on the head, their partner should call out the name of another group member so the target changes again.

6. If the partners of Member B and Member C do not call another member's name in time, then Member A will gently bop them on the head with the newspaper. The person who was bopped will become the person holding the newspaper.

Reminders and precautions

Be aware of any issues for group members being bopped on the head. If there is worry that this could be dangerous, then the game can be changed to bopping them on the shoulder or arm instead.

Debriefing

None.

40

 15 minutes

 10–20
(it is better to play this game with an even number of participants; if there is an odd number, then one group member should be selected to be a judge)

 None

Reminders and precautions

None.

Debriefing

None.

Calling names competition

Objectives

Allow group members to get to know each other better and test their reaction times.

How to play

1. Group members should be divided into two teams.
2. The teams should sit in two straight lines facing the members of the opposing team.
3. Each team is allowed to have 20 seconds to discuss and decide the order for the team members to stand up (i.e., who is the first, second, and so on to stand up).
4. The game facilitator should then say "1, 2, 3, go!", and the assigned first member of each team should stand up immediately and quickly yell out the name of the standing member of the opposite team (the assigned first member of the opposite team). The game continues with the assigned second members, and so on.
5. Step 4 should be repeated until all the members in each team have participated.

41

15–20 minutes

10–12

None

Remember the names with four beats

Objectives

Help group members quickly remember the names of other members.

How to play

1. Group members should be asked to introduce themselves or should be wearing name tags.

2. Group members should practice the four beat tempo and actions while sitting in a circle:

   First beat: slap both hands on thighs;
   Second beat: clap;
   Third beat: snap the fingers of the left hand; and
   Fourth beat: snap the fingers of the right hand.

3. Once the group is performing the actions, the game facilitator or a designated group member should start the game by "passing the beat" to another member.

4. To pass the beat to another member, they should call the name of another group member on the third beat and specify a beat number (1, 2, 3, or 4) on the fourth beat.

5. The member whose name has been called should respond by repeating their own name on the next beats until reaching the beat number they were designated. For example, if the number called on the fourth beat is 3, then they need to say their name on the second beat, third beat, and fourth beat, all while keeping the beat with the actions above.

6. In the next set of beats, the new member should call someone else's name on the third beat and a number on the fourth beat, and the process continues repeating Steps 3 and 4.

7. The game can be played with the entire group until everyone's name has been called. Members who miss the beat or do not say their name the correct number of times lose, and Steps 3 and 4 can be started again.

Reminders and precautions

1. This game is not suggested to be played with too many group members.

2. This game can be played online.

Debriefing

None.

42

 15 minutes

 10–20
(it is better to play this game with an even number of participants; if there is an odd number, then one group member should be selected to be a judge)

 A large bed sheet

Hide and call names

Objectives

Allow group members to get to know each other better and test their reaction times.

How to play

1. Group members should be divided into two teams.

2. The teams should sit in two straight lines facing the members of the opposing team.

3. The game facilitator should invite two members to help hold up the large bedsheet between the two teams, thus blocking their view of the other team.

4. Each team will then have approximately 20 seconds to discuss and decide the order for the members to stand up (i.e. who is the first, second and so on to stand up).

5. To start the game, the first assigned member of each team should stand up on their side of the bedsheet. The game facilitator should then say "1, 2, 3, go!", and the two members holding the bed sheet should drop it. The standing member on each team should then quickly yell out the name of the standing member of the opposite team (the assigned first member of the opposite team). The game continues with the assigned second members, and so on.

6. Step 5 should be repeated until all the members in each team have participated.

Reminders and precautions

The bedsheet should be thick enough to prevent team members from seeing and knowing who is standing.

Debriefing

None.

43

 15 minutes

 10–20
(it is better to play this game with an even number of participants; if there is an odd number, then one group member should be selected to be a judge)

 None

Finding the spy

Objectives

Allow group members to get to know each other better and test their reaction times.

How to play

1. Group members should be divided into two teams.

2. Each member should be assigned a number and should not let the members of the opposite team know. For example, if a team has 10 people, then the numbers assigned should be from 1 to 10.

3. Team members should line up in a random order in a straight line facing the members of the opposing team.

4. To start the game, the game facilitator should say "Where is the spy?", to which the group members should reply "Which spy?" The facilitator should then reply "Spy 00X (such as 007)". The members of the two teams who are not assigned the number 7 should kneel down immediately. The remaining two members with the assigned number 7 should remain standing and point at each other while shouting the name of the opposing member. The fastest and most accurate member wins.

5. Everyone will stand up again, and the game facilitator will start another round.

Reminders and precautions

None.

Debriefing

None.

The members of the two teams who are not the number called should kneel immediately. The members with that number should remain standing and point at each other while shouting the name of the opposing member.

44

 20–25 minutes

 10–20

 A large nylon string ball

Weave a spider web

Objectives

Enhance understanding among group members, increase interactions, and create a collective feeling.

How to play

1. Group members should stand in a circle and get to know each other's names.

2. The game facilitator will suggest a theme (e.g., group members' names, hobbies, favourite singer, etc.). One member should hold the nylon string ball and share something about themselves related to the theme. Then, while holding the end of the nylon string, the member needs to say the name of another member and throw them the nylon string ball keeping hold on the end.

3. The second member who catches the ball needs to share something about themselves related to the theme. After sharing, they should hold onto a point on the string and say the name of another member before throwing them the string ball. This should continue until all members are holding on to part of the string, thereby creating a spider web between them.

4. The game facilitator can change the theme to understand more about group members.

5. Once the spider web is tight enough, group members can lower the web and invite one group member to sit or lie on top of the web. Other group members should cooperate and work together to raise the member who is sitting or lying on the spider web.

Reminders and precautions

1. Encourage members to throw the nylon string ball to relatively quiet members.

2. Step 5 should only be executed if the spider web is tight and the group members are collectively strong enough to hold up the weight of the group member sitting or lying on the web. Safety should be a priority.

Debriefing

1. Explain how the spider web represents the interpersonal network within the group and how each group member is connected to others.

2. Discuss how building the web highlights the importance of building up a mutual-aid network and helping each other.

45

 20–25 minutes

 At least 15–20

 Sheets of paper with the nine squares on it as shown (one sheet for each participant), pens

Please sign for me

Objectives

Help members get to know more about each other.

How to play

1. Group members should answer the nine questions on the paper on the line in each square.

2. Over the next 20 minutes, each member needs to find other members who have the same answer for one of the questions and invite them to sign their names inside the brackets below the answer. A member can only sign another member's paper once.

3. The group member who is able to collect nine signatures should then be asked to introduce their new friends.

4. Optional: Using the sheets with the signatures, the group can play "Bingo", whereby the game facilitator will draw slips of paper with members' names one by one. If a group member has that member's name in one of their squares, then they can cross out that box. The first member who has three in a row wins.

Reminders and precautions

None.

Debriefing

Talk with the group members about how they feel about the links they have made with other people who have similar backgrounds or interests.

My Name: _____

Favourite colour	Favourite fruit	District of residence
_____ ( )	_____ ( )	_____ ( )

Birthday month	Favourite flower	Favourite sport
_____ ( )	_____ ( )	_____ ( )

The last digit of your mobile phone number	Favourite pop singer	Favourite country you like to visit
_____ ( )	_____ ( )	_____ ( )

46

 20 minutes

 At least 8–10

 A4 paper (one sheet per participant), pens, adhesive tape

Knowing you, me, and others

Objectives

Allow members to get better acquainted with each other.

How to play

1. Each member should be given a piece of A4 paper. They need to write their name or nickname in the middle of the paper, then write down some information about themselves at the four corners of the paper (such as their favourite country to visit, your district of residence, favourite fruit, and favourite genre of music).

2. After writing all the above information, members should stick the paper on their chest using adhesive tape or they can simply hold the paper in front of their chest. Then, all members should stand up and move around to meet other members, shake hands, and share their information.

3. The game facilitator should remind members not to chat too long with one member (ideal time with one member is 2–3 minutes).

Reminders and precautions

This game can be played online by organising two members in virtual breakout rooms for 2–3 minutes for each round.

Debriefing

Help members reflect on how comfortable they felt introducing themselves and how well they listened to the other group members talk about themselves.

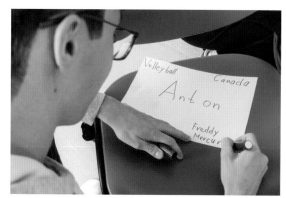

47

 20–25 minutes

 No limit

 A4 paper (one sheet per participant), pens

Paper airplanes

Objectives

Help members get to know the characteristics and personalities of other group members.

How to play

1. Each member should be given an A4 paper and asked to write some words in the middle describing their own character, personality, or strengths. However, members should not write about their appearance and need to keep what they have written hidden from others.

2. After writing, they should fold the paper into an airplane and stand to one side of the venue. After the group members close their eyes, the game facilitator should count "1, 2, 3", and each member should throw their airplane out at the same time.

3. Group members should then open their eyes. The game facilitator should then ask each member to pick up an airplane or they should all be asked to pick up an airplane at the same time.

4. Members will then unfold and read the information on the paper. They then need to guess who the owner of the airplane is.

5. Optional: To keep the game going for longer, when a member reads the information on the paper, instead of saying the name of who they think it describes, they can write their guess on the bottom of the paper. Then they should fold it again and repeat the process of flying, picking up, reading, and guessing. This can be repeated for any number of rounds before the guesses are read out loud.

Reminders and precautions

1. Members should not make the paper airplanes with a sharp corner.
2. This game should be played in a large area.
3. Members should be cautious not to bump into others while picking up the airplanes.

Debriefing

Help members understand how others perceive them in relation to their true characteristics.

48

 20 minutes

 16–20

 A4 paper (one sheet per participant), pens

Superluminal running

Objectives

Allow group members to get to know each other, enhance mutual understanding, and build up team spirit.

How to play

1. Group members should be divided into several teams. The number of teams and members in each team depends on the total number of participants. Each team needs to have an equal number of members. For example, if the total number of participants is 30, they can be divided into three teams with 10 members in each team, two teams of 15, or five teams of 6.

2. Members of each team should stand behind each other at one side of the venue — the start line. The lines for each team should be parallel so they all start from the same place.

3. Each team member should be given an A4 paper, and they should write their name in the middle.

4. As the game starts, the first member of each team should run or walk quickly to the other side of the venue, turn around, and run or walk quickly back to the starting line. While running, members need to keep the sheet of paper on their chest without using their hand to touch or hold it. It will need to be held in place by the force of their forward momentum. If the paper drops, the member has to stop, pick up the paper, and go back to the start point to run again.

5. Before running, each member needs to shout "I'm XXX (their name) and I'm a superluminal runner". After a member has made it back to the start after running, the next member of their team should go. The fastest team to finish wins.

6. The game can be changed by asking members to write other words on the paper and to shout these words before running, such as the slogan of the team, the group's name, personal strengths, or areas for personal improvement.

Reminders and precautions

1. This game should be played in a large area or venue.
2. Members should pay attention to their personal safety while running and do warm-up exercises before the game starts.

Debriefing

None.

49

 20 minutes

 10–20

 Pieces of individually wrapped candy (five pieces per participant)

Never say "I"

Objectives

Enhance mutual understanding between members and help them get to know more about each other.

How to play

1. Each member should be given five candies.

2. Each member should then move around and talk to different members to get to know more about them (e.g., their name, family, interests, etc.).

3. During the chat, members cannot say "I". If a member says "I", then they have to give a piece of their candy to the other person.

4. When the game finishes, those who end up with the most candy wins. Members can then eat the candies together after the game.

Reminders and precautions

1. Members must not chat too long with one member. They should find more members to chat and change their partner every 2–3 minutes.

2. It is not suitable to use candy with nuts if anyone in the group has a nut allergy. Thus, the facilitator should check with the members about this before playing the game.

Debriefing

Discuss the strategies members used to avoid saying "I" during their conversations.

3

Group Cooperation
and Cohesion Games

50

 20 minutes

 8–10

 Balloons

Protecting the balloon

Objectives

Create a relaxing atmosphere and strengthen cooperation among group members.

How to play

1. Group members should form a circle by holding hands.

2. The game facilitator should toss a balloon into the circle. The group members need to cooperate and use any part of their bodies to keep the balloon from hitting the ground. The only condition is that they need to continue holding hands during the game.

3. To increase difficulty, group members can be instructed to not use their hands or arms to touch the balloon.

4. When group members are familiar with the game, more balloons can be added into the circle.

5. If there are a lot of group members, then it may be necessary to divide the group into smaller teams to compete with each other.

Reminders and precautions

1. This game is suitable for families and people with learning difficulties.

2. This game is not suitable for elderly group members or people who are uncomfortable with physical contact.

Debriefing

1. Ask members to share their feelings about successfully protecting the balloons in the circle.

2. Help members understand or become aware of how cooperation plays a crucial role in finishing this task together.

51

 20–25 minutes

 8–10 per team

 Balloons, stickers, pens

Balloon riddles

Objectives

Create a relaxing atmosphere and strengthen cooperation among group members.

How to play

1. Group members should be divided into teams. Each team should then be asked to blow up balloons according to a required number.

2. Each team will then be given some assigned stickers with words written on them. These words can form an assigned message, such as the group name, the organisation name, the name of the game facilitator, the slogan of the group, theme of the activity, or some other message the game facilitator wishes to deliver. The game facilitator can also give the teams additional stickers with words not related to the assigned message, and the teams will then need to choose the correct stickers. The game facilitator can also give blank stickers to the team and ask the team members to write the assigned words on the stickers.

3. The game facilitator should then tell the members the desired message, and each team will then need to quickly find and stick the correct stickers on the balloons and arrange the balloons in the right order.

4. The fastest team to line up the message and balloons in the right order wins.

5. The game facilitator can also ask the team members to read out the words on the balloons to enhance members' understanding of the assigned messages.

6. Lastly, each team can pop the balloons together to create organised chaos or strengthen the bonds between team members.

Reminders and precautions

The sound of popping balloons may frighten some group members or disturb others in the environment. Thus, this game is best played in a spacious venue and the facilitator should ensure that everyone is comfortable with popping the balloons.

Debriefing

Help members have a clear understanding of the messages written on the stickers.

52

 15–20 minutes

 8–10 per team

 Balloons, obstacles

Balloon train

Objectives

Strengthen group cooperation and increase communication between group members.

How to play

1. All group members should stand in a straight line facing the back of the member in front of them. Each member should blow up a balloon and place it in front of their chest. One by one, each member should step forward to trap their balloon between their chest and the back of the person in front of them.

2. Within a certain time limit, the whole group needs to work together to walk around the venue, avoiding obstacles set by the game facilitator (e.g., chairs) and get to a finishing point without dropping any of the balloons. While playing the game, group members are not allowed to use their hands to touch or hold the balloons.

3. If there are a lot of group members, the game can be changed to become a small team competition. The team that finishes first without dropping any balloons wins.

Reminders and precautions

1. This game should be played in a spacious venue to prevent teams from bumping into each other and to have the obstacle course be spread out.

2. This game is not suitable for group members uncomfortable with physical contact.

3. Members should be cautious when running to avoid falling.

4. The game can be changed by placing the balloons at different body parts (e.g., between shoulders or sides of hips) to increase the level of difficulty.

Debriefing

Help members become aware of how they had to work together to adjust the speed and movements of the group to complete the task.

53

 20–25 minutes

 8–10 per team
(it is better to play this game with an even number of participants; if there is an odd number, then one group member should be selected to be a judge)

 Chairs, balloons, toothpicks

Reminders and precautions

1. Some members may be scared of popping the balloons.

2. Ensure that team members and the leaders fully understand the rule that they are not allowed to stand up and that their hips have to remain stuck to the chairs.

3. The facilitator should prepare many balloons to ensure that the game can last a certain amount of time, especially if the balloons seem to pop easily or if the teams are very quick.

Debriefing

None.

Pop the balloons

Objectives

Strengthen the spirit of participation and enhance group cooperation.

How to play

1. Group members should be divided into two teams (Teams A and B). Half of the members in each team should be assigned the number 1, and the other half should be assigned the number 2.

2. Chairs should be arranged in two parallel lines. Members with the same number will sit on the same line next to the member of the opposite team. That is, the seating arrangement in one line should be A1, B1, A1, B1, etc., and the arrangement for the opposite line should be B2, A2, B2, A2, etc. Thus, each A1 should be facing a B2, and each B1 should be facing an A2.

3. Each team should select one member as the team leader who will hold a toothpick. The leaders, one at each end, should sit between the two lines facing towards the middle.

4. When the game starts, the game facilitator will throw a balloon in between the two lines. Members of the two teams will have to use their hand to hit the balloon towards their respective team leaders, all while staying seated.

5. When the balloon reaches the end, the team leader should use the toothpick to pop it (also staying seated on the chair). The teams get one point for each balloon they can pop.

6. The game facilitator can then throw another balloon, and the game continues. The team with the highest number of points wins.

54

20–25 minutes

16–20
(with 8–10 in a team; it is better to play this game with an even number of participants; if there is an odd number, then one group member should be selected to be a judge)

Newspaper, adhesive tape, chairs, balloons

Reminders and precautions

Members should pay attention to their safety while running and swinging the stick.

Debriefing

Help members describe the effects of group support while they were trying to hit the balloon.

Hit the ball with paper sticks

Objectives

Allow members to warm up and enhance group cooperation.

How to play

1. Group members should be divided into two teams with an equal number of members.

2. Each member should be assigned a number. For example, if the team has eight members, the number assigned to the members should be from 1 to 8.

3. Each team should be given two pieces of newspaper and adhesive tape to make two paper sticks.

4. The members of each team should then stand side by side behind a line on one side of the playing area and face the opposing team. A certain distance should be kept between the two teams. A chair (representing the goal) should be placed on either side of the line.

5. A balloon and one paper stick from each team (the second stick made by the team is kept for reserve) should be placed in the middle of the floor.

6. When the game starts, the game facilitator calls a number. The member of each team with this number quickly runs to the middle and picks up their team's stick to hit the balloon into their goal (i.e., pass through under the chair). Members can only use the stick and not any part of the body to touch or hit the balloon.

7. If neither member scores, the game facilitator will call another number. The original two members should then put down the stick and return to their team on the sidelines, while the next member called should immediately go to replace the previous member where they were last standing before picking up their team's stick and hitting the balloon towards the goal. This should continue until a team scores a goal.

8. The team that gets the most goals wins.

55

 20–25 minutes

 16–20
(with 8–10 in a team; it is better to play this game with an even number of participants; if there is an odd number, then one group member should be selected to be a judge)

 Balloons

Reminders and precautions

1. Members should be cautious for their safety while moving or running.
2. The safest and fastest way is to put the balloon between the hips of the two members and put their hands on one's shoulders while moving. If necessary, tips can be given to the teams that are struggling to finish.
3. This game may not be suitable for group members who are uncomfortable with physical contact.

Debriefing

Help members share their cooperation methods and where they think the best place to hold the balloon was.

Quick pass

Objectives

Allow members to discover the best cooperation method.

How to play

1. Group members should be divided into two teams (can be three teams if there are a lot of participants) with an equal number of members.
2. The playing area needs to be marked with two lines to represent the start and endpoints.
3. The members of each team should find a partner within their team. All groups of the team should then line up behind the start point.
4. Each group should be given a balloon. When the game starts, the first group of each team should quickly move the balloon from the starting point to the endpoint and then come back to the starting point. The balloon should be stuck between the two partners. While moving, the two members are not allowed to use their hands to hold the balloons but can use any other parts of their bodies. If the balloon hits the ground while they are moving or running, they have to stop to pick up the balloon and start again.
5. The fastest team to have all of their groups finish wins.

56

 20–25 minutes

 16–20
(with 8–10 per team; it is better to play this game with an even number of participants; if there is an odd number, then one group member should be selected to be a judge)

 Balloons, chairs

Three in contact, one to hit

Objectives

Enhance group cooperation.

How to play

1. Group members should be divided into two teams with an equal number in each team.

2. Members of one team should go to the left-hand side of the game area, and those of the opposing team should go to the right-hand side. A chair should be placed on both sides of the playing area.

3. The members of each team must use three of the four points of the body (two hands and two feet) to touch the floor with their chest facing up.

4. When the game begins, a balloon will be placed in the middle of the game area.

5. Members of each team should then move and use only one point of the body (three points should be touching the floor) to hit the balloon.

6. The team that can make the balloon hit the chair of the opposite team wins.

Members must keep three out of the four points of the body (two hands and two feet) touching the floor.

Reminders and precautions

Members should pay attention to their safety.

Debriefing

Help members share their feeling of success through cooperation.

57

 20 minutes

 12–16
(with 6–8 per team; it is better to play this game with an even number of participants; if there is an odd number, then one group member should be selected to be a judge)

 None

Invisible volleyball

Objectives

Enhance group cooperation.

How to play

1. Group members should be divided into two teams with an equal number of members in each team. If there are more than 16 group members, then the others can be the audience/judges.

2. One team should get ready at the left-hand side of the game area, while the opposing team should go to the right-hand side. The teams should then decide who will play specific volleyball positions: the setter, the outside hitter, and the opposite hitter.

3. When everyone is ready, the game facilitator will tell them that they are going to play volleyball with an invisible ball.

4. The team that performs better and acts out a better volleyball match will be the winner. This can be decided by the game facilitator, a designated judge, or the audience, who can vote for the winning team.

Reminders and precautions

Members should pay attention to their safety to avoid injury.

Debriefing

1. Help members share their feelings about their devoted involvement in the activity.

2. Help members learn to freely and genuinely express themselves through play.

58

 20 minutes

 10–15

 Hula hoop (may also use circular ropes or paper circles)

Hula hoop pass

Objectives

Enhance trust and team spirit within the group.

How to play

1. The game can be played in a big group with a set finishing time or as a competition between two teams.

2. Members should stand in a circle, facing inward and holding hands. A hula hoop should be placed within the chain (so the arms of the group members pass within the hoop).

3. When the game begins, members should move their bodies to pass the hula hoop from one member to another while still holding hands.

4. The game ends when the hula hoop gets back to the start point.

5. To increase the level of difficulty, the game can be changed so that two hula hoops are being passed at the same time. Teams will lose if the two hula hoops meet at one member's body. This change can motivate members to pass the hula hoop as quickly as possible, thus creating a more exciting atmosphere.

Reminders and precautions

1. This game should be played in an open and flat area.
2. The size of the hula hoop should fit the body size of the members.
3. Members should be cautious not to lose balance while passing through the hula hoop to avoid falling.
4. This game is not suitable for group members who are uncomfortable with physical contact.

Debriefing

Help members share their feelings about the level of cooperation in the team.

59

 20 minutes

 10–15 per team

 Baby formula cans or oatmeal cans

Pass the can

Objectives

Build group cohesion and team spirit.

How to play

1. This game can be a competition between different teams or played as one team with a time limit.

2. Members should sit in a circle on the floor, facing the centre. They should be given an empty baby formula or oatmeal can without the lid.

3. Team members should then try to pass the can to the person next to them using only their feet. No other body parts can be used.

4. To make the game more challenging, two cans can be passed around at the same time.

5. Another way to play this game is to ask members to remove their shoes before playing. After they have finished the game, they will need to run to find and put on their shoes as fast as possible.

6. If it is not possible to get a baby formula or oatmeal can, then a shoe or a ball may be used.

Reminders and precautions

This game is not suitable for group members wearing a dress or skirt.

Debriefing

Help members share the differences between having and not having help or support from other members when passing around the can.

60

 20 minutes

 10–15 per team

 Hand-made paper rings

Foot to foot

Objectives

Develop group cohesion and cooperation.

How to play

1. The same method of passing around the objects by feet will be used as that in Game 59. It can be played as a competition between different teams or as one team with a time limit.

2. Members should sit in chairs arranged in a circle, facing the centre. They should be given a paper ring.

3. Team members should then try to pass the ring to the person next to them using only their feet. No other body parts can be used.

4. To make the game more challenging, two rings can be passed around at the same time.

Reminders and precautions

This game is not suitable for group members wearing a dress or skirt.

Debriefing

Help members share the differences between having and not having help or support from other members when passing around the rings.

61

 20–25 minutes

 8–10

 Any objects to be passed (e.g., pen, rubber band)

Pass through the arch

Objectives

Strengthen cooperation within the group, enhance interactions, and create a positive atmosphere.

How to play

1. Group members should be asked to take off their shoes and socks and sit next to one another on the floor.

2. When the game begins, the game facilitator will give an object (e.g., a pen, a rubber band) to the first member. Then, members should pass the object around the circle using only their feet.

3. After the object has reached the last member, everyone except the first member should make an arch pose. The first member should then crawl on the floor, passing under all of the arches.

4. The game can be played as one group with a set finishing time or it can be played as a competition between two teams.

Reminders and precautions

This game is not suitable for group members wearing a dress or skirt. It is also not suitable for members who are uncomfortable with physical contact.

Debriefing

None.

62

 15–20 minutes

 10–20

 None

Circle sit

Objectives

Strengthen cooperation and team spirit within the group.

How to play

1. Members should stand in a circle, facing the same direction with both hands holding onto the shoulders of the member in front of them.

2. When the game facilitator says "start", the members must work and cooperate together to slowly sit on the knees of the member behind them. All members need to keep holding onto one another in a circle without anyone falling or having any gaps.

3. When all members are able to sit still safely, the game facilitator will ask them to raise both of their hands, clap hands, or sing together.

Reminders and precautions

This game is not suitable for group members wearing a dress or skirt. It is also not suitable for group members who are uncomfortable with physical contact.

Debriefing

Help members reflect on the importance of cooperation with one another and on the feeling of accomplishing a task as a team.

Members should slowly sit on the knees of the member behind them and then reach out one hand.

63

 20–25 minutes

 12–16

 None

Hands and feet

Objectives

Strengthen group cooperation and test members' reaction times.

How to play

1. This game can be played in a big group with a set time limit or as a competition between two teams.

2. Members need to cooperate with one another and listen to the game facilitator's instruction about the number of hands and legs that should be touching the floor for each team.

3. The game facilitator should designate a "counting area". When they say "# hands and # feet!", group members need to immediately put the correct number of hands and feet on the floor in the counting area. For example, when the game facilitator says "16 hands and 8 feet!", the group needs to determine how to position everyone so this number of hands and feet are on the floor in the counting area.

4. An alternative is if each hand or foot is simply regarded as one point. When the game facilitator says "# points", all members need to cooperate to put the right number of the points on the floor in the counting area.

Reminders and precautions

This game is not suitable for group members wearing a dress or skirt.

Debriefing

None.

64

 20 minutes

 20–24
(it is better to play this game with an even number of participants; if there is an odd number, then one group member should be selected to be a judge)

 None

Reminders and precautions

1. When the members of the Interfering Team are jumping or doing actions, members should be careful to avoid injury.
2. The game facilitator needs to stop the game if the situation becomes too aggressive or chaotic.

Debriefing

Discuss the importance of developing an effective communication method in the group.

Jump and see

Objectives

Enhance group communication and cooperation.

How to play

1. Group members should be divided into two teams (A and B) with an equal number in each team. Team A should be further divided into two equal sub-teams: the Action Team and Guessing Team. Team B will be the Interfering Team.

2. The members of the Interfering Team should stand in between the members of the Action Team and the Guessing Team.

3. When the game begins, the game facilitator should tell the Action Team a category (e.g., fruit, sports). The members of the Action Team are not allowed to speak and must use their body language to act out one item in that category (each member should choose a different thing to act out). The Guessing Team members will need to guess the category based on the Action Team's movements.

4. Members of the Interfering Team should make loud noises or make a lot of movement, such as jumping and waving their hands, in order to try and block the sight of the Guessing Team members and hinder them from guessing the correct category.

5. The time used by the Guessing Team members to guess the category correctly should be counted.

6. For the next round, the roles of Teams A and B are reversed.

7. The team which guesses the correct category fastest wins.

65

 20–25 minutes

 4–5 per team

 Rope or paper strips

Grab the tail

Objectives

Enhance cooperation and team spirit within the group.

How to play

1. Group members should be divided into multiple teams. Members of each team should form a line and place their hands on the shoulders of the member in front of them. The last member should be given a rope or paper strip, which they should tuck into their waistband or back pocket of their pants (it should not be fastened too firmly). This is the team's tail.

2. When the game begins, the members of each team should run around to try and grab the tail of the other teams, while avoiding having their own tail grabbed. Teamwork is essential.

3. When a team grabs the tail of another team, these two teams then need to combine into one team, with the losing team members standing in the front. The combined team should then continue to move around to grab the tail of the remaining teams.

4. The game ends when all teams combine to form a long dragon with only one tail left.

5. Alternatively, when a team has their tail grabbed, they are eliminated and should stand on the side-lines to cheer for the other teams. The last team standing wins.

Reminders and precautions

The facilitator should pay attention to the personal safety of each group member and ensure that the game does not become too chaotic. This game is not suitable for group members who are uncomfortable with physical contact.

Debriefing

Help members understand that success does not depend on the efforts of a single person but on the complementary and cooperative efforts of the whole team.

66

 20 minutes

 12–16
(6–8 per team; it is better to play this game with an even number of participants; if there is an odd number, then one group member should be selected to be a judge)

 A ball or a plastic water bottle

Reminders and precautions

1. Facilitators should pay attention to the personal safety of each group member while they are running and competing.
2. First-aid materials should be prepared in advance.
3. This game should be played in an open and large venue.

Debriefing

Help members understand the importance of complementary and cooperative efforts.

Fighting for the ball

Objectives

Strengthen group cooperation and test group members' reaction times.

How to play

1. Group members should be divided into two equal teams. Each member should be assigned a number. For example, if the team has six members, then the numbers assigned should be from 1 to 6.

2. Members of each team should then stand side by side along a line marked on the floor and face the opposing team. A certain distance should be kept between the two teams. A ball (or a plastic water bottle) should be placed on the floor between the two lines.

3. When the game begins, the game facilitator will say a number. The member of each team assigned with that number should then quickly move forward to grab the ball. The member who is able to grab the ball and run back to their team area behind the line gets one point. However, if the opposing member touches any part of their body before they are in their team's area, they will lose one point. If they choose to drop the ball before the opposing member touches them and they still touch them, then the opposing team loses one point. If they drop the ball and the opposing team member does not touch them, then the ball is still in play and can be picked up by either member. If either member gets a point or loses a point, then they can return to their team's area. If neither member gets a point, then the game facilitator will call another number. That group member will then replace the previous group member in the game, and the previous member will return to their team.

4. Step 3 should be repeated until a team reaches a certain score. The game facilitator may use a mathematical question (using addition, subtraction, multiplication, or division) and ask the two teams to calculate the result. Once the teams find the calculated number, they have to follow Step 3 to play the game. (For example, if the math equation $9 - 3 \times 2$ is given for them to solve, then the member assigned with the number 3 should move forward to grab the ball and run back to their team area, as explained in Step 3.)

67

20 minutes

16–20
(8–10 per team; it is better to play this game with an even number of participants; if there is an odd number, then one group member should be selected to be a judge)

None

Reminders and precautions

None.

Debriefing

Help members understand the difference between having and not having strategies in group cooperation.

Follow the number

Objectives

Allow members to warm up and strengthen group cooperation.

How to play

Method 1:

1. Group members should be divided into two teams with an equal number of members. The members of each team should sit in a line side by side facing the opposing team.

2. When the game begins, the facilitator will call a number. Each team should have the correct number of members standing up immediately. For example, if the game facilitator calls "5", then five members of each team have to stand up.

3. The team that has the correct number of persons standing the fastest wins.

Method 2:

1. After dividing into teams, each team member should be assigned a number. For example, if the team has eight members, the number assigned should be from 1 to 8.

2. When the game begins, the game facilitator will call a number. The teams should determine the correct members to stand up to total this number. For example, if the game facilitator calls "20" (and there are 9 members in the team), then members assigned the numbers 3, 4, 6, and 7 (or 1, 2, 8, and 9) should stand up together.

3. The fastest team to have the correct combination of people standing wins.

4. The game facilitator can also change the mathematical operation and ask members to calculate the number result.

68

 15 minutes

 6–8 per team

 Table tennis balls, a table

Blow across

Objectives

Enhance team spirit within the group.

How to play

1. The game facilitator should draw a line to divide the table into two sides.

2. Group members should be divided into two teams. Members of each team will stand at the two different parts of the table and are not allowed to enter the area of the other team.

3. After placing a table tennis ball on the centre line on the table, the members of the two teams should try to blow and make the ball move to the other part of the table.

4. If members of one team can make the ball move to the other part of the table and fall on the floor, they can get one point.

5. Members can only use their mouths to blow the ball around.

6. To add excitement, multiple balls can be placed on the table at the same time.

Reminders and precautions

None.

Debriefing

1. Help members understand that every member is important in the game and that they have to cooperate and hold onto their own positions.

2. Help members become aware of the importance of having the same goal and the effective way to have self-defence and attack the opponent.

69

 20–25 minutes

 20–30
(with 6–8 per team)

 None

The best in the world

Objectives

Enhance group communication and cooperation.

How to play

1. Group members should be divided into two or three teams.

2. The game facilitator should announce an adjective of a characteristic, such as "the tallest...", "the shortest...", "the biggest...", etc.

3. Each team will then need to pick a representative from their team who they think is the best example of that characteristic. That member should go to the facilitator. For example, if the facilitator says "the shortest...", teams might send up someone who is the shortest in height, has the shortest hair, has the shortest arms, etc. They have to guess what characteristic the adjective is describing.

4. The team with the member who is the best representative of the characteristic wins.

Reminders and precautions

This game can be played online using breakout rooms for groups.

Debriefing

None.

70

 20–25 minutes

 6–8 per team

 None

The collectors

Objectives

Enhance group communication and cooperation.

How to play

1. Group members should be divided into two or three teams.

2. The game facilitator will then ask each team to collect some objects from their members, such as two pairs of spectacles, three belts, four pens, or two watches.

3. The quickest team able to collect all the assigned objects and accurately hand them to the game facilitator wins.

Reminders and precautions

This game can be played online.

Debriefing

None.

71

 20–25 minutes

 6–8 per team

 None

Question and guess

Objectives

Enhance group communication and cooperation.

How to play

1. Group members should be divided into teams, with six to eight members each.

2. Each team needs to decide a person, place, or thing for another team to guess (e.g., a historical figure, a country, a kind of fruit, or a name of a street, etc.).

3. The other team should ask 10 yes or no questions to narrow down what it could be. For example, "Is it someone famous?" After asking the 10 questions, the team asking the questions needs to guess what it is.

4. The game facilitator should also set a time limit.

5. After the first round, another team should pick a person, place, or thing, and another team should ask questions and guess.

Reminders and precautions

This game can be played online.

Debriefing

Help the group members learn different techniques for asking questions and narrowing down the options.

72

 20–25 minutes

 8 per team

 The materials depend on the assigned challenges

Reminders and precautions

1. Challenges should vary and incorporate multiple skills, such as spelling, singing, aiming to hit a balloon, distance throwing, etc. However, challenges should be coordinated based on the target group to avoid unnecessary danger.

2. The challenges should not be related to any money betting.

3. Facilitators should pay attention to the challenges involving movement or significant competition, which may cause arguments or conflicts.

Debriefing

Help members understand and reflect on the group's communication methods that worked well as well as how conflicts were handled.

How much to risk?

Objectives

Enhance group communication, develop team spirit, and recognise each individual's strengths.

How to play

1. Group members should be divided into teams, with a minimum of two teams. Each team starts with 1,000 points.

2. The game facilitator should set up different kinds of challenges, such as finding a certain number of items around the venue in 10 seconds.

3. Each team is allowed to use 1 minute to discuss and decide if they believe they can complete the challenge or not and how many points they want to bet on being able to complete it (at least 100 points for each challenge). If a team thinks they can complete the challenge, they should then designate a representative or group of representatives to complete the challenge. If they complete the challenge, their team will get the betted points. However, if they fail the challenge, then the number of points they bet will be deducted.

4. If none of the teams believes that they can complete the challenge, then the game facilitator should change to another challenge.

5. The team with the most points wins.

73

 20–25 minutes

 12–20

 Paper, pens

Pass the facial expression

Objectives

Create a joyful atmosphere, enhance team cooperation, and highlight the limitations of non-verbal communication.

How to play

1. The game facilitator should choose five to six group members who will play the game, while the other members will be in the audience. Alternatively, another way to play the game is to divide members into two or three teams and let them have a competition. However, ideally, having an audience is better.

2. The group members playing the game should form a line parallel with the audience all facing the same direction. They can choose to stand or sit, but they cannot turn around to look at the member behind them until told to do so.

3. The game facilitator should prepare some facial expression words, such as furious, excited, happy, sad, and write each word on a small piece of paper.

4. The game facilitator should then ask the member at the back of the line to choose one paper and look at the word. They should then tap the shoulder of the member in front of them so they turn around to look at them. Then, they should execute the facial expression or action to let that member guess the word, but they cannot speak or make any sound. Members should continue to pass the expression word along to the member at the front of the line.

5. When the member at the front of the line receives the expression, that person must try to guess the word represented by that facial expression. The game facilitator can help them with suggestions if necessary.

6. Team members who guess correctly can then move to the back of the line (to become the first person making the expression). Team members who guess incorrectly are eliminated from the game and should sit down in the audience, while a new person from the audience should move to the back of the line (to become the first person making the expression). Then Steps 4–6 can be repeated to continue the game.

Reminders and precautions

Each group member should be given the opportunity to be the first person in line making the facial expression, the person at the end of the line to guess, in the middle of the line to pass the expression, and in the audience.

Debriefing

Help members understand that a message passed by many people may deviate from the original and only relying on non-verbal communication or body language may not be able to convey the accurate meaning of the message through such a chain.

74

15–20 minutes

16–20
(8–10 per team; it is better to play this game with an even number of participants; if there is an odd number, then one group member should be selected to be a judge)

Pretzel sticks, cheese ring (or other ring-shaped snack)

Cheese ring pass

Objectives

Enhance the spirit of group cooperation and teamwork.

How to play

1. Group members should be divided into two teams with an equal number of members in each team. Each team should form a line all facing the same direction.

2. Each member should be given a pretzel stick and place one end in their mouth.

3. A cheese ring will be given to the first member of each team to put around their pretzel stick. While still holding the pretzel stick with their mouths, the first member should then try to pass the cheese ring onto the pretzel stick of the member behind them. They should not use their hands.

4. The faster team to pass the cheese ring to the last member in the line wins.

5. Alternatively, the pretzel sticks and cheese ring can be replaced with a straw and a rubber band, respectively.

Reminders and precautions

None.

Debriefing

Help members understand the importance of mutual adjustments when cooperating with one another.

75

 15–20 minutes

 8–10 per team

 Any object (such as a balloon, key, pen)

Body conveyor belt

Objectives

Enhance the spirit of group cooperation and teamwork.

How to play

1. Group members should be divided into several teams with eight to ten members. Each team should form a line facing the same direction.

2. Members should close their eyes and cannot speak or make noises.

3. When the game begins, the facilitator will give an object to the first member of each team. The first member should then use both hands to hold the object and pass it over their head to the member behind them without dropping it. Members cannot turn around to pass the object. If the object is dropped, then the team needs to start passing the object from the first member again.

4. The fastest team to pass the object to the last member wins.

Reminders and precautions

Heavy objects should not be used as this could lead to injuries if the object is dropped.

Debriefing

Help members share how they cooperated with their eyes closed and without any verbal communication.

76

 20 minutes

 10–15

 Blindfolds

Dangerous trip

Objectives

Enhance mutual trust within the group.

How to play

1. Before the game starts, the game facilitator should prepare numbers on slips of paper to draw.

2. Members should be asked to randomly draw a number. After knowing their own number, all members will be blindfolded.

3. Once blindfolded, members should move around, call their own number, and then line up with their hands on the shoulders of the member in front according to the order of the numbers.

4. This process can be timed and each round they can try to line up faster.

5. To add difficulty, the game facilitator can add some obstacles, such as chairs or small tables, around the venue. Members will need to avoid the obstacles to line up. This can be timed and the facilitator can also count the number of times group members touched the obstacles.

Reminders and precautions

Facilitators should pay close attention to each group member's safety to help them avoid tripping while blindfolded.

Debriefing

1. Help members share their feelings about playing the game blindfolded as well as their views about trusting other group members.

2. Discuss how to enhance communication and trust with other members.

77

 20 minutes

 12–15

 None

Trust rocking

Objectives

Help members relax and develop trust within the group.

How to play

Method 1:

1. Group members should form teams of three. One member ("A") should stand between the other two members ("B" and "C"). Member B should face Member A, while Member C should stand behind Member A.

2. Member A should close their eyes, place their arm across their chest, and relax. While standing firmly, Members B and C should then put their hands on the shoulders of Member A.

3. To start the game, Member B should use both hands to gently push on the shoulders of Member A so they lean backwards slightly. Member A should not move their legs.

4. While Member A is leaning backward, Member C should use both hands to press on the shoulders of Member A so that they push forward slightly. Again, Member A should not move their legs. This gentle pushing will create a rocking sensation for Member A as they tilt backward and forward with the help of Members B and C.

5. After several rounds of rocking, the three members should change their roles.

Method 2:

1. All group members should stand in a circle facing the centre. The facilitator should designate one member ("A") to stand in the centre. All other members should then move forward to let their hands slightly touch the shoulders of Member A.

2. Member A should close their eyes, place their arms across their chest, and relax. Member A should not move their legs.

3. Members should then begin to use their hands to gently push Member A's shoulders and make them lean forward, backward, to the left, or to the right. Members need to make sure that they can hold Member A firmly before they push.

4. If Member A can relax and trust all other members more, then they will feel comfortable rocking their body.

Reminders and precautions

1. Members must remember to push slowly and gently. Facilitators should pay close attention to the member at the centre to prevent them from falling.

2. This game is not suitable for group members who are uncomfortable with physical contact.

Debriefing

1. Help the rocking member to share their thoughts or concerns about trusting other group members.

2. Discuss how each person can communicate better with each other during the game to enhance trust.

78

 20–25 minutes

 12–16
(with 6–8 per team)

 Blindfold, newspaper, adhesive tape, chair, nylon rope

Knock off the hat battle

Objectives

Enhance the spirit of group cooperation and teamwork.

How to play

1. Group members should be divided into two teams, and each should select one member to be the warrior. They should also make a hat and stick (sword) out of newspapers.

2. The warrior should then put on the paper hat, hold the sword, and be blindfolded.

3. The game facilitator should use four chairs and nylon ropes to make a square area which represents the battlefield.

4. When the game begins, the warrior of each team should be brought into the battlefield. All other members are not allowed inside the battlefield.

5. All members outside the battlefield will use their voices to tell or give instructions to their warrior to use the sword to gently knock off the hat of the other team's warrior.

6. The team whose warrior knocks off their opponent's hat wins.

Reminders and precautions

1. Facilitators must be aware of the safety of the team members acting as the warriors as they may fall while they are blindfolded.

2. Group members should be reminded to be gentle when they swing their swords.

Debriefing

1. Ask group members to explain their communication methods and strategies used to win.

2. Help the warriors share their thoughts about trusting their team members.

79

 20 minutes

 12–16
(with 3–4 per team)

 6–8 table-tennis balls,
3 boxes or strings

Reminders and precautions

None.

Debriefing

1. Help members reflect on their communication skills.
2. Discuss how the throwing member felt about their team's strategy and the level of trust they felt.

You say, I throw

Objectives

Strengthen cooperation and trust within the group.

How to play

1. Group members should be divided into two or three teams. Each team should select one member to throw the balls.

2. A box should be placed three to four steps behind the throwing member. Other members need to face the selected member and stand three to four steps in front of them.

3. The group members will need to verbally instruct the throwing member how to toss the balls behind them and into the box.

4. The team that can get the most balls into their box wins.

5. If no table-tennis balls are available, then small plastic balls or hand-made newspaper balls may be used. If hand-made newspaper balls are used (i.e., balls that will not bounce), then string or a piece of paper can be used to mark the box area.

80

 15 minutes

 12–16
(with 6–8 per team)

 Paper balls made
out of newspaper,
blindfolds

Paper ball attack

Objectives

Strengthen cooperation and trust within the group.

How to play

1. Group members should be divided into two teams with six to eight members in each.

2. All members should help to make as many paper balls as they can from the newspaper.

3. Members of each team should stand in a line facing the opposing team, maintaining a certain distance between the two lines.

4. Each team should select a team member to be the attacker. This member will be blindfolded. The attackers of each team should kneel in front of their own team, still facing the opposing team. The paper balls should be placed on the floor around the two attackers.

5. When the game begins, each attacker has to find ways to pick up the paper ball and then throw to hit the attacker of the opposite team. If the paper ball hits the body of the attacker of the opposite team, then they get one point. Only the attackers can touch the balls, but the other group members should verbally instruct the attackers where the balls are, where to throw to hit the other attacker, as well as how to avoid getting hit.

6. The team with the most points wins.

Reminders and precautions

The game facilitator should monitor the safety of the attackers as they will be blindfolded and could fall while moving around.

Debriefing

Help members share the effective communication methods they used to help the attacker and how these methods allowed the attacker to trust their team members.

81

20 minutes

12–16
(with 3–4 per team)

A4 size paper

Step over the obstacles

Objectives

Strengthen cooperation and mutual trust within the group.

How to play

1. Group members should be divided into several teams, with three to four members in a team. The game facilitator should set a starting point and a finishing point. "Obstacles" can also be set by placing pieces of A4 paper on the ground.

2. Each team will need to send a representative to walk from the starting point to the finishing point blindfolded.

3. The walking member will need to listen to their team members and rely on their instructions to know how and where to walk. They will need to avoid stepping on any of the paper obstacles. If they do step on an obstacle, then they will need to start over again from the starting point.

4. The quickest team to reach the finishing point wins.

Reminders and precautions

Attention should be paid to the safety of the blindfolded representative who may fall while blindfolded.

Debriefing

1. Discuss the communication methods the teams found the most effective.

2. Ask the walking member to talk about the level of trust they felt with their team.

82

 20–25 minutes

 6–8 per team

 Blindfolds (1 per team), 1 treasure, chairs (or other obstacles that do not cause safety issues)

Treasure hunt with a twist

Objectives

Strengthen cooperation and team spirit within the group.

How to play

1. Group members should be divided into several teams, with six to eight members in a team. Each team should select one member to hunt for the treasure. This member will be blindfolded and will rely on other team members to instruct them where to walk or move around.

2. However, other team members are not allowed to use the words forward, backward, left, right, or stop to instruct the blindfolded member. They have to come up with different terms for these. For example, if animal names are used, then dog could be used to replace forward, cat could replace backward, tiger could replace left, lion could replace right, and elephant could replace stop. Each instruction is equivalent to one step, two instructions are equivalent to two steps, and so on. For example, "dog, dog, dog" means they should take three steps forward. Repetition of animal names between the teams should be avoided.

3. Each team should have its own route with a starting and finishing point. The starting point and the finishing point should not be too far apart. Otherwise, listening to their team's instructions could be difficult for the blindfolded member.

4. The game facilitator should place some obstacles along the route of each team (e.g., chairs) and a treasure (e.g., water bottle or paper cup) at the finishing point.

5. Each team can also assign one member to stand next to the blindfolded member to ensure their safety. However, the assigned member is not allowed to provide any instructions.

6. When the game starts, the blindfolded member of each team should walk from the starting point to the finishing point according to their team's instructions. Other members have to shout out the instructions together behind the starting point. The team wins when their blindfolded member is the first to get the treasure.

Reminders and precautions

Attention should be paid to the blindfolded member to avoid falling.

Debriefing

1. Ask the blindfolded member to share their feelings about trusting their team and if they could or could not follow their instructions.
2. Help members reflect on ways to strengthen team cooperation to assist the blindfolded member.

83

 20 minutes

 6–8 per team

 None

Searching with signals

Objectives

Increase and enhance interactions between group members and strengthen group cooperation.

How to play

1. Group members should be divided into two teams or several teams, with six to eight members in a team. Each team will have one minute to discuss how to recognise their team members without using their voices. They can set up some specific cues or signals.

2. Then the team members should spread out around the venue, close their eyes, and stop speaking.

3. Each team then needs to find all of its members and stand in a straight line within the time limit. After finding all of their team members, the team needs to cheer or shout a slogan. The quickest team wins.

Reminders and precautions

The game facilitator should monitor the group members as they move around with their eyes closed and could bump into each other.

Debriefing

Help members consolidate the most effective ways of finding or recognising their team members.

84

 15 minutes

 20
(it is better to play this game with an even number of participants; if there is an odd number, then one group member should be selected to be a judge)

 None

Partner hunt

Objectives

Increase and enhance interactions between group members and strengthen group cooperation.

How to play

1. This game is similar to Game 83. The difference is that the game will be played in pairs rather than a team.

2. Group members should find a partner and pick out identifying features that they will be able to feel. For example, they can try to remember the size of their partner's wrists or hands, if they are wearing a watch or ring, the length of their sleeves or type of fabric, and so on.

3. The partners should then spread out. After all of the group members close their eyes, the game facilitator can also change their positions.

4. When the game starts, group members should move around, feeling the hands, wrists, and accessories of others they come in contact with until they find their partner. They cannot speak or make noise during this time.

5. Once they think they have found their correct partners, then the pair should raise their hands in the air for the facilitator to check. When time is up, everyone should open their eyes to see if they are correct.

Reminders and precautions

This game is not suitable for group members who are uncomfortable with physical contact.

Debriefing

Discuss some of the ways group members effectively found or recognised their partners.

85

 15 minute

 10–12

 Chairs

Voice recognition

Objectives

Strengthen the bonds between group members and help them get familiar with other members' names and voices.

How to play

1. The chairs should be arranged in a circle facing inward. Each group member should sit in a chair.

2. The group facilitator should choose one member to start ("A"). They should stand in the middle of the circle and close their eyes. The facilitator can lead Member A around so they do not remember the order of the group members still sitting.

3. Member A should then slowly walk towards one of the sitting group members. The facilitator can help guide them once they decide the direction they want to go. Then Member A should stand in front of one group member with their back to them.

4. Member A should then ask who that member is. That member can use a fake voice to answer or give an incorrect name. Member A will then need to guess who they are as quickly as they can.

5. If Member A guesses correctly, then the other member will be the next one to be in the centre of the circle. If Member A guesses incorrectly, then they can either keep asking questions about who they are or they can walk and stand in front of another member to start again.

6. Alternatively, instead of standing in front of the other group members while guessing, Member A can sit on the lap of the person. However, this style should only be played if all of the group members already have a close relationship. It is not suitable for group members who are uncomfortable with physical contact.

Reminders and precautions

The game facilitator should be aware of where the guessing member is moving to avoid falls.

Debriefing

Help members share any change they felt in the relationships and distance between group members after playing.

86

 20–25 minutes

 10–15

 Tables, chairs, A4 white paper, coloured pens (each participant needs to have a piece of A4 white paper and 2–3 coloured pens)

Share feelings by drawing together

Objectives

Encourage members to express their feelings and enhance members' ability to share and accept feedback.

How to play

1. Each group member should be given a piece of paper and two or three coloured pens.

2. Group members should sit in a circle and write their names in the middle of their paper.

3. Each member will then have 30 seconds to reflect on their feelings towards the group or towards the activity or programme they have just joined. Then, they will have 1 minute to start drawing an image expressing these feelings.

4. When the game facilitator says "stop", every member needs to pass their drawing to the person sitting to their right.

5. Members will have 10 seconds to think about how they could add to the other person's drawing. Then, they will have 20 seconds to draw.

6. Steps 4 and 5 will be repeated until everyone's drawings have gone all the way around the circle (and each group member has added to every other member's drawing).

Reminders and precautions

None.

Debriefing

1. Help members share their feelings about how others have added to their drawings.
2. Discuss any similarities or differences between the feelings and emotions that were drawn by others.

4

Problem-solving Games

87

 20–25 minutes

 10–15
(if there are many participants, then they can be divided into teams)

 A long circular rope or nylon string

Build the shapes

Objectives

Help members learn how to solve problems together as well as strengthen team cooperation and cohesion.

How to play

1. Group members should stand in a circle and hold a part of a long circular rope or nylon string. They should then close their eyes.

2. The game facilitator will call out a shape (e.g., circle, triangle, square, rectangle, star, etc.). Keeping their eyes closed, members should try to build that shape by talking and touching.

3. If the game is played with one group, then the facilitator can set a time limit to complete the shape. If there are multiple teams, then the game can be played as a competition in which the fastest team to make the correct shape wins.

4. The game facilitator can finish the game by asking members to build a heart shape. After completing the shape, members can put the rope or nylon string in the heart shape on the floor.

5. Members can then be asked to stand or sit around the heart shape to discuss their personal expectations or wishes concerning the group or share some encouraging words to other group members.

Reminders and precautions

None.

Debriefing

Help members reflect on the communication pattern, leadership style, decision-making method, cooperation, and cohesion in the group.

The heart shape can be used for sharing encouraging words or how each member feels towards other group members.

88

 15–20 minutes

 10–15
(if there are many participants, then they can be divided into teams)

 None

Reminders and precautions

1. It is best to only play this game one or twice to avoid losing the sense of initial excitement and challenge.
2. This game may not be suitable for group members who are uncomfortable with physical contact.

Debriefing

1. Help members share their feelings about completing the game.
2. Discuss the different ways used to communicate and how each person adjusted to and accepted different opinions throughout the game.

Untangle the arms

Objectives

Help members learn how to solve problems together, strengthen the relationships within the group, and develop team cooperation.

How to play

1. Group members should stand in a circle and reach both hands into the centre.
2. They should then grab onto the hands of other members so that everyone's arms and hands are crossed and locked together. However, members must avoid grabbing both hands of the same person. Members also cannot hold the hands of the members on their immediate left or right.
3. The whole group must then try to determine how to untangle their arms in order to form a circle without unlocking their hands.
4. Groups can be timed or the game can be played as a competition between teams.
5. To make the game more challenging, members can be told not to speak.

89

 20–25 minutes

 10–15
(if there are many participants, then they can be divided into teams)

 None

Inward to outward

Objectives

Help members learn how to solve problems together, strengthen the relationships between group members, and develop team cooperation.

How to play

1. Group members should stand in a circle, facing inward and holding hands.

2. All members must keep holding hands throughout the game.

3. As a team, they must work together to find a way to turn around so everyone is facing outward from the circle. Notably, members should not have their arms crossed when they are facing out.

4. Solution: Any two members can hold up their linked arms to make an "arch". One member from the opposite side of the circle should then lead the rest of the circle to pass under the "arch". When all members have passed, they will be facing outward while still holding hands. The game facilitator should allow members to have a suitable amount of time to discuss and test different solutions before giving hints and explaining how to do it.

Reminders and precautions

None.

Debriefing

1. Help members share their feelings about completing the game.

2. Discuss the different ways used to communicate and how each person adjusted to and accepted different opinions throughout the game.

90

 15 minutes

 10–15

 Short straws (the number of straws must be equal to the number of participants)

Straw challenge

Objectives

Develop group problem-solving and cooperation skills.

How to play

1. Group members should stand in a circle.

2. Each member should be given a short straw. The facilitator should assist group members so they are holding the straw with their neighbour, each of them using only one finger of one hand.

3. Once there is a straw connection between each group member around the circle, the game facilitator should instruct members to do different actions, such as rotating, jumping, or kneeling down.

4. Members must move together to complete the action without dropping the short straws.

Reminders and precautions

None.

Debriefing

Help members explain how they had to work together to complete the tasks effectively and emphasise the importance of mutual cooperation and team spirit.

91

 20–25 minutes

 6–8 per team

 Short straws (the number of straws must be equal to the number of participants)

Flip with straws

Objectives

Enhance communication and cooperation between group members.

How to play

1. Group members in each team should stand in a circle facing the centre.

2. Each member should be given a short straw. The facilitator should assist group members so they are holding the straw with their neighbour, each of them using only one finger of one hand (similar to Game 90).

3. As a team, they must work together to find a way to turn around so everyone is facing outward from the circle while not dropping any of the straws (similar to Game 89). Notably, members should not have their arms crossed when they are facing out.

4. If any straw drops during the game, then members will have to repeat Steps 2 and 3 and start again.

5. To increase the difficulty level, members can be asked to keep quiet throughout the process.

6. The solution to this game is the same as that for Game 89, with the added difficulty of the delicate balance of holding the straws.

Reminders and precautions

None.

Debriefing

Help members explain how they had to work together to complete the tasks effectively and emphasise the importance of mutual cooperation and team spirit.

92

 20–25 minutes

 6–8 per team

 Two pieces of newspaper per team

Step by step

Objectives

Teach group members to cooperate together to solve problems.

How to play

1. Group members should be divided into teams, each with six to eight members. Each team should be given two pieces of newspaper. The game facilitator should set a start point and an endpoint. The teams should stand at the start.

2. To start the game, each team should place the first piece of newspaper on the floor, and all group members should then stand on it.

3. Then, they should put the second piece of newspaper down towards the finish, and each group member should then move from the first piece to the second piece. The piece they were standing on previously should then be moved closer to the finish using their feet (will require them to push it on the floor from person to person around one side of the other piece).

4. Step 3 should be repeated until they reach the finish.

5. Team members are not allowed to step off of the newspaper. If a member touches the floor, then the team has to start over. They are also not allowed to tear the newspaper.

6. The quickest team to reach the finishing point wins.

Reminders and precautions

This game may not be suitable for group members who feel uncomfortable with physical contact as they may have to stand close together or hang on to each other to avoid falling off the newspaper.

Debriefing

Help members reflect on their communication and cooperation methods as well as their feelings about their team after playing the game.

93

 20–25 minutes

 12–16

 None

Stand up together

Objectives

Develop group problem-solving and cooperation skills.

How to play

1. Group member should find a partner to form teams of two to start.

2. Each pair should sit on the floor back to back with their arms linked. They must then try to stand without using their hands or arms to push up from the floor.

3. When a pair is able to do this successfully, then they should combine with another pair to form a team of four. The four members of this new team should repeat Step 2 to continue playing the game.

4. The game continues by increasing the number of members in the team to make it more challenging.

Reminders and precautions

1. The game facilitator must prioritise the safety of each group member as falling may occur while trying to stand.

2. This game is not suitable for group members with back pain or who feel uncomfortable with physical contact.

Debriefing

Discuss the importance of group cooperation and help each group member explain how they contributed to solving a problem together.

94

 20–25 minutes

 16–20
(4 per team)

 None

Hands only

Objectives

Strengthen problem-solving abilities and the spirit of cooperation within the group.

How to play

1. Group members should be divided into teams of four. Each team should then discuss how they can arrange themselves to only have their hands touching the floor (no feet or other parts of the body).

2. The quickest team to find a way to do this successfully wins.

3. Solution: The four team members should first go into a plank or push-up pose. Then, they should shift around so each person has their feet positioned on the back of another person, forming a square. Teams should be allowed to test different solutions before the game facilitator provides hints or the solution.

Reminders and precautions

This game is not suitable for members with back pain or who are uncomfortable with physical contact.

Debriefing

1. Help members share their feelings about finishing the game.

2. Discuss each team's communication strategy and how different opinions were dealt with in a cooperative manner.

95

 20–25 minutes

 6–8 per team

 Many pieces of newspaper

All in the boat

Objectives

Enhance group problem-solving capabilities and develop their understanding of group cooperation.

How to play

Method 1:

1. Each team should be given a large piece of newspaper. This represents a boat that every team member must get on.

2. Each team member needs to stand in the boat, and their feet cannot touch the floor.

3. When the game starts, the game facilitator will tell them that they have been hit by a big wave and part of their boat is destroyed. All of the members will need to move closer together, and the facilitator will tear off part of their newspaper. Members of each team then need to cooperate and work out a way to ensure all members can still stay in the boat. Each members' feet need to touch the remaining newspaper (meaning no one can be carried or held up).

4. If a team member steps off their boat (i.e., the newspaper), then that team is eliminated.

5. Repeat Step 3. The team with all of its members still standing on the newspaper wins.

Method 2:

1. Follow Steps 1 and 2 of Method 1.

2. When the game starts, the game facilitator should ask a question. The teams that answer correctly the fastest will avoid the big wave and can choose the team that the wave will hit. When this happens, part of their newspaper will be torn off as in Method 1.

3. When the game finishes, the team that has the largest area of the newspaper intact wins.

Reminders and precautions

1. Group members should be reminded to avoid dangerous actions or positions which could cause them or another member to fall.

2. This game is not suitable for members who feel uncomfortable with physical contact.

Debriefing

1. Help members understand the power of working together to solve the difficulties.

2. Ask members to reflect on how each member of the group contributed.

3. Discuss the relationship between support and cooperation as well as how this relationship relates to success and failure.

96

 20–25 minutes

 6–8 per team

 A large piece of newspaper or plastic sheet

Flip the raft

Objectives

Help group members develop problem-solving skills, strengthen mutual cooperation, and learn different communication styles.

How to play

1. Each team should be given a large piece of newspaper or plastic sheet. This will represent a raft.

2. All team members need to stand on the raft. They should then try to flip it over so the bottom side is facing up. During the process, all members must stay on the raft and should not touch the area outside the raft. Otherwise, they will need to start over.

3. The fastest team to flip their raft with everyone still in it wins.

Reminders and precautions

1. Group members should be reminded to avoid dangerous actions or positions which could cause them or another member to fall.

2. This game is not suitable for group members who feel uncomfortable with physical contact.

Debriefing

1. Help members understand that success comes from collective cooperation and participation.

2. Discuss the importance of the preparatory work before attempting a task as well as how understanding members' expectation, strengths, and limitations can help make the team successful.

97

 20–25 minutes

 6–8 per team

 Newspaper, adhesive tape

The tower

Objectives

Encourage members to pay attention to teamwork and enhance group cooperation.

How to play

1. Group members should be divided into several teams, each with six to eight members. Each team should be supplied with a pile of newspapers and one or two rolls of adhesive tape.

2. Members of each team should work together to use the newspaper and adhesive tape to build a tower within a set time limit. If a team's tower falls, then they must start over.

3. The team that builds the highest tower wins.

Reminders and precautions

1. Members should be encouraged to voice their opinions while working together.

2. The game facilitator should watch for any team members being ignored or excluded and encourage them to participate.

Debriefing

Help members share their communication and cooperation styles as well as their feelings about their teammates after finishing the game.

98

 20–25 minutes

 10–12

 None

Blind walk

Objectives

Help break barriers in communication between group members and enhance group cooperation.

How to play

1. Group members should stand in a circle, holding hands and facing outward.

2. The game facilitator should designate one member to stand inside the centre of the circle and be the guide. All other group members need to close their eyes and stay quiet.

3. When the game starts, the guide can use any means (except touch) to instruct all members to walk together. They should keep holding hands at all time as they walk the route instructed by the guide.

4. The facilitator can also choose to set up a course for them to follow or add obstacles.

Reminders and precautions

1. The game facilitator may need to remind group members to slow down and to walk carefully to prevent them from falling when moving too fast.

2. The guide should avoid instructing members to walk to places that have potential dangers (e.g., areas with limited space or sharp corners, or routes that cross uneven ground).

Debriefing

1. Encourage members to talk about their communication styles and help them understand that if barriers or difficulties in communicating with one another exist, then misunderstandings can occur.

2. Discuss how better communication skills can be developed to complete complex tasks.

99

 20–25 minutes

 9–12
(with 3 per team)

 Blindfolds or eye-covering cloth

Body coordination

Objectives

Help members learn how to cooperate and communicate.

How to play

1. After being divided into groups of three, each team should be given two blindfolds.

2. Each team member can only use one of these three body parts: eyes, hands, or mouth. For example, the member who can only use their eyes will not be allowed to use their mouth or hands (i.e., taste or touch) but can see and speak, while the member who can only use their hands will be blindfolded and not allowed to use their mouth (i.e., see or taste). The member who can use their mouth will be blindfolded and not allowed to use their hands (i.e., see or touch).

3. The game facilitator should then request each team to perform an action or series of actions, such as eating something or blowing up a balloon. Each team will need to talk and coordinate with each other to accomplish the tasks.

4. The first team to accomplish the task correctly wins.

Reminders and precautions

None.

Debriefing

1. Help members understand that everyone has different strengths and weaknesses which can be used to help the whole group.

2. Discuss the importance of cooperation in a group.

100

 20–25 minutes

 10–12

 Many straws, a few table-tennis balls

Straw track

Objectives

Help members learn how to cooperate and enhance team spirit.

How to play

1. Each group member should be given one straw. They should then line up in two straight lines facing each other, with each group member standing across from another group member.

2. Holding their straw with both hands, each group member should make a track with the group member across from them. The track should be able to hold a table-tennis ball and allow it to roll from one end to the other. Each pair of group members should then connect their tracks with the tracks on either side, thus forming one long track.

3. Members will then need to pass a table-tennis ball along the track from a starting point to a finishing point without touching the ball with anything other than the straws.

4. If the initial track is not long enough to reach the finishing point, then after the table-tennis ball passes over one track, those two group members will need to run to the other end of the track and form a new section of track. This should be repeated until the track extends to the finishing point wins.

5. If the ball falls off of the track during the process, then members need to go back to the starting point again.

6. If the game is played as a competition between two teams, then the quickest team to finish passing the ball to the finishing point wins.

Reminders and precautions

None.

Debriefing

Help members learn how to find an effective way to work together and adjust to one another when they are cooperating and solving problems together.

About the Editor, Contributors, and Game Collaborators

Editor

Dr Ping Kwong Kam obtained a B.Soc.Sci. (Hons) degree in social work from the University of Hong Kong, M.Sc. in Advanced Social Work Studies from the University of Edinburgh, and PhD from the University of Sheffield, United Kingdom. He joined the City University of Hong Kong in 1989 and is currently an Associate Professor in the Department of Social and Behavioural Sciences. He has been teaching social work courses for 32 years. He is a two-time winner of the Teaching Excellence Award (1994 and 2008), winner of the Faculty of Humanities and Social Sciences Contribution to Learning Award (1999), and winner of the Knowledge Transfer Award (2012 and 2019), all awarded by the City University of Hong Kong. He has also worked as a social work practitioner and service supervisor. He is a registered social worker in Hong Kong and has worked in the field of community development, children and youth service, service for older people, and staff training and development for social work practitioners. He specialises in teaching social work courses. His areas of teaching and research include team building and group work skills, group games, community development, macro social work practice, working with special needs groups, community organising skills, foundations of social work, social work education, social work values and belief, social gerontology, powerlessness issues, empowerment practice, and the EPS model in social work practice. He has published widely in these fields, including books and many articles in international refereed journals.

Contributors

Ping Kwong Kam	Associate Professor, Department of Social and Behavioural Sciences, City University of Hong Kong
Yau Kuen Lau	Honorary Lecturer, Department of Social Work and Social Administration, The University of Hong Kong
	Chairman, Challenge Course Association of Hong Kong, China (2002–2004)
Kwok Wing Chan	Supervisor, The Boys' & Girls' Club Association of Hong Kong
Fai Kuen Leung	Level 3 Instructor of Low Event, High Event, Abseiling, Challenge Course Association of Hong Kong, China

Game Collaborators

The 100 group games selected for this book were drafted by Dr Ping Kwong Kam and the following 43 graduates from the Bachelor of Social Sciences in Social Work (Full-time) Programme, City University of Hong Kong. Each game was edited, organised, revised, and finally compiled by Dr Ping Kwong Kam.

2004–2007 Cohort

Yin Ting Au	Fung Wah Chan	Ho Chit Alson Chan
Kit Ying Chan	Wai Ching Chan	Wing Yi Chan
Shuk Man Chiu	Nga Lai Choi	Wing Ching Choi
Yim Fong Chung	Yuk Yu Lau	Suk Ching Leung
Tsz Yan Wong	Yip Hung Wong	

2006–2009 Cohort

Hoi Ying Chan	Chik Fat Cheng	Chung Yin Cheung
Man Ha Chiu	Yim Ting Fu	Sze Man Fung
Kai Pong Ho	Yan Tsz Hazel Kam	Sze Ho Ku
Oi Nga Lau	Wai Kam Lau	Wing Chi Lau
Choi Fung Lee	Kwok Kam Lee	Ka Lo Leung
Yue King Liu	Sai Ho Ng	Wai Wen Ng
Wing Man Ng	Chau Mui Tam	Kai Yeung Tam
Shuk Ching Tang	Wing Han Tsang	Chi Lun Wong
King Kuen Wong	Wing Sze Wong	Toi Yung Yau
Kwan Tai Kimble Yeung	Man Yeung	